Y0-EHY-208

Volume 21 

Advances in Librarianship

Volume 21

Advances in Librarianship

Edited by

Irene Godden

The Libraries
Colorado State University
Fort Collins, Colorado

Academic Press

San Diego London Boston New York Sydney Tokyo Toronto

This book is printed on acid-free paper. ∞

Academic Press
a division of Harcourt Brace & Company
525 B Street, Suite 1900, San Diego, California 92101-4495, USA
http://www.apnet.com

Academic Press Limited
24-28 Oval Road, London NW1 7DX, UK
http://www.hbuk.co.uk/ap/

International Standard Book Number: 0-12-024621-X

PRINTED IN THE UNITED STATES OF AMERICA
97 98 99 00 01 02 BB 9 8 7 6 5 4 3 2 1

Contents

Contributors

Numbers in parentheses indicate the pages on which the authors' contributions begin.

Stephanie Rogers Bangert (91), St. Mary's College of California, Moraga, California 94575

Terence K. Huwe (1), Institute of Industrial Relations, University of California, Berkeley, Berkeley, California 94720-5555

Holley R. Lange (47), Colorado State University Libraries, Fort Collins, Colorado 80523

Diane Lunde (73), Colorado State University Libraries, Fort Collins, Colorado 80523

Margaret Small (25), Associate Librarian, University of New England, Armidale 2351, Australia

Sara R. Williams (73), University Libraries, University of Colorado at Boulder, Boulder, Colorado 80523

B. Jean Winkler (47), Colorado State University Libraries, Fort Collins, Colorado 80523

Preface

For this, the twenty-first volume of *Advances in Librarianship*, and a volume that includes a cumulative subject index, it seems appropriate to take a look both backward and forward.

Advances in Librarianship was begun in 1970; the first editor was Melvin Voigt. He was sole editor for five volumes, and then he shared the editorship with Michael Harris for two more volumes. Michael Harris was then editor until 1981. He was succeeded by Wesley Simonton, who served as editor for volumes 12 through 14, until 1986. There then was a gap during which no volume appeared, until I began my editorship with Volume 15 in 1991.

Today *Advances* has almost 700 continuing orders worldwide, 350 of which are from the United States, 138 from the international division, 178 from the United Kingdom, and 26 from Australia. This wide distribution has been fortunate, in that having *Advances* well known in major areas of the world tends to attract a wider base of authors.

In the first volume of *Advances* (1970), Melvin Voigt defined the purpose and scope of the annual as follows:

> There has long been a need for a continuing series to provide scholarly reviews of the rapidly changing and advancing field of librarianship, a series which would select subjects with particular current significance to the profession and provide an analysis of the advances made through research and practice. *Advances in Librarianship* is planned and designed to fill this need. It will present critical articles and surveys based on the published literature, research in progress, and developments in libraries of all types. Its authors are experts who have played major roles in the advancement of the subjects they review.

He continued:

> The aim of *Advances in Librarianship* is to document changes and their effects—to provide a forum for the review and analysis of librarianship as it exists today as well as its potential for tomorrow.

This description still applies to *Advances* today. Melvin Voigt also said that the series "intended to provide a permanently useful reference volume which will document the progress of librarianship as it changes its methods and scope and perhaps even its objectives," so *Advances*, while looking forward, is also creating a historical record.

I have been asked what, in my opinion, have been the most important "advances" in the field as reflected in what has been published in the annual in the last five to ten years or so. I believe that there have been several: First, I think that the field of library science has matured, in that there seems to be more hard research done and reported. This may be partially due to the influx of grant funds from the information science side of the field, as well as to the increased pressure that universities have put on their library/information science school faculties to produce research similar to that of their colleagues in other disciplines. Another "advance," at least from my vantage point in the United States, is increased awareness of international developments in the field. Every single volume that I have edited has included at least one or two articles on library and library science developments in other countries, articles on universal developments as seen from an international perspective, and articles that have featured one or more international authors. Incidentally, the Internet has made it much easier to contact authors worldwide or to be contacted by them. I picked up several ideas for articles, for example, from the various list servers. Inquiries from prospective authors also now tend to come by e-mail and almost never by "snail mail."

Another macro advance has been in the rethinking of the very basis of the profession (see, for example, Pertti Vakkari, "Library and Information Science: Its Content and Scope" in Volume 18), and the resultant revamping of existing organizations, including libraries, library systems, and as a result, library science education programs. Several articles cover these subjects, including one in Volume 20 that reported on a grant-funded effort at the University of Michigan to create a model program to support professional training for library leaders in the digital age. Not coincidentally, the new name for the former School of Information and Library Studies is now simply School of Information.

In addition to these shifts, there have, of course, been very significant "advances" in specific areas of the field. The growth in preservation activities that were formerly based in a few libraries with valuable special collections is a fairly dramatic example of this. We now have nationally coordinated efforts to preserve our common heritage, and advances in technology that support activities such as mass deacidification, mass microfilming, and digitization.

Advances in other traditional areas of library services are also not hard to find. To give but a few examples, acquisitions has been redefined as acquisitions and access, cataloging has been transformed by standardization and automation, and catalogers along with computer specialists are involved in developing standards for a version of "metadata," a core set of elements being developed to describe networked resources.

While traditional interlibrary loan still exists, it is being supplemented, and in part replaced, by independent electronic access to indexes as well as to text, coupled with new methods of document delivery such as direct fax, direct mail, and file transfer. And, as the library itself is no longer solely a place where one comes to retrieve a book or periodical article, traditional reference services are being rethought and reshaped.

We in the library profession are also being forced to "advance" by the enormous growth in electronic communications, which in turn affects the publishing process. With many journals now available in electronic format, is the library indeed still the best agent for providing access to our researchers? And if we are, how do we convince our administration and faculty of this? For example, I have been looking for someone to do an article on the potential impact of new bundled electronic products such as "Engineering Information Village," a place where researchers can react to each other and access published materials as well as research in progress, all for a standard access fee. What will this type of development mean for libraries? The economics of the question are by no means clear, given that even if the library or a consortium of libraries can negotiate a better price for the package, the infrastructure that needs to exist to get this "better" price is enormously expensive. From my own personal perspective as a library administrator, I do of course see a future role for libraries and librarians. I see an expansion of our instructional function (the Engineering Information Village does have an icon "ask a librarian") plus a possible role, if indeed this develops, when universities will start to retain copyright and self-publish, bypassing the commercial publishers, at least for some scholarly publications. Our skills in organizing and making available for use information on complex subjects would be valuable here.

There are many more examples of current and potential advances in the field as we move toward the "digital library" of the future. Harvard University recently hosted an entire conference, for example, on the topic Economics of Digital Information and Intellectual Property, and in January 1997, the Coalition for Networked Information cosponsored a conference on digital libraries calling for research on such topics as:

- evaluation methods and user testing
- hypertext and hypermedia
- image, graphical, GIS, and multimedia information
- indexing and classification
- information storage and retrieval
- metadata and knowledge representation
- scanning and digital preservation
- World Wide Web

- user interfaces, visualization, browsing, and searching
- user behavior and information needs analysis, etc.

The greatest difficulty continues to be in capturing all these developments in a format suitable for publishing in *Advances in Librarianship*.

The five authors whose chapters appear in this volume deal with a subset of the questions concerning the library and information profession: What is the role of libraries as institutions in information communities? In the planned "virtual university"? How are our mission statements dealing with those questions, if at all? What is the future of bibliographic control? How are ongoing developments, such as in preservation, affecting other areas of librarianship?

Huwe discusses the role of information in organizations, the destabilizing effects of technology upon traditional organizational structures, and the blurring of disciplinary boundaries. Guiding themes and narratives about the use of information in organizations are mapped and evaluated. He ends with specific recommendations challenging librarians to focus their core skills during this time of organizational change, and suggests potential migrations through increasingly fluid organizational patterns. His three specific recommendations include a call to migrate "with skillfulness," to create "virtual communities," and to revamp professional organizations.

Small investigates the roles libraries have or have not been playing in the development of the virtual university in both Australia and the United States. The concept of virtual university is defined, and specific projects are described. The author also describes library services provided by virtual universities today and outlines approaches librarians could and should take to ensure that students' information needs are not given short shrift in the rush to create the new programs.

Lange and Winkler, in their chapter "Taming the Internet: Metadata, a Work in Progress," give an excellent and very useful overview of national and international efforts to create access/index points, or "data about data," for the enormous amount of information available in electronic format via the Internet. As libraries and other information communities move toward their own version of the digital library, this is "must" background reading.

Lunde and Williams trace the history and outlook for collection development/management in United States research libraries, and detail the interdisciplinary nature of collection management and preservation. The origin and growth of preservation activities are also described in some detail. The authors end with a call for preservation practitioners to create a unified philosophy for their discipline, an intellectual structure that will provide justification and funding for the deliberate and organized preservation of our historical records.

Last but not least, Bangert analyzes a set of California college and university library mission statements and describes the prevalent values and vision, and their relationship, or lack thereof, to the mission of the parent institutions. It is of interest to note that Bangert, like Huwe, calls upon academic librarians to express in clearer terms why the culture of the library is valuable and to be explicit about the meaning and the value of their services and resources. Specific approaches are suggested.

Libraries and the Idea of the Organization

Terence K. Huwe
Institute of Industrial Relations
University of California at Berkeley
Berkeley, California 94720-5555

I. Introduction

Information management and access are central concerns for society and for all types of organizations. The rapid evolution of information technology has brought new pressure to bear on traditional disciplines and professions, and it is challenging the assumptions we hold about organizations and our roles in them. Just as multi- and hypermedia blur the lines of formerly static access technologies such as books and sound recordings, so also is the structure of organizations changing. The workplace itself is a living laboratory for competing organizational models. Despite their expertise, managers and business consultants labor in the same tradition of trial and error as does basic science.

As information managers, librarians are at the epicenter of this process. But while their viewpoints on the meaning of information and community are important, they are often overlooked. Long the pioneers of the qualitative uses of information and inheritors of a humanistic tradition, librarians have been joined in the past 25 years by a host of other professionals who are also addressing the problems of information collection, access, and counsel. This is the direct result of technological change, which has triggered convergence in academic disciplines and management theory and among information practitioners of every stripe.

This chapter is expanded from lectures given at the Doreen B. Townsend Center for the Humanities at the University of California at Berkeley and the Centennial Congress of the International Federation for Information and Documentation (FID) in The Hague, the Netherlands. The FID conference focused on the changing paradigms underway in all areas of information management. The lecture topic "Changing Organizations" was a major theme of the conference. Research about the various approaches of information

0065-2830/97 $25.00

managers in corporate firms uncovered several larger issues which bear special attention by information professionals.

First, digital media, which can be reduced to binary code and transferred infinitely, is limited only by available computing power and imagination (Negroponte, 1995). This in itself is leading to the disintegration of the boundaries between varieties of expertise. In the workplace, "digital convergence" is rewriting the structure of business, causing both opportunity and dislocation (Yoffie, 1996).

Second, organizational design and theory have not kept pace with the evolution of technology. Many individuals within organizations, even highly trained managers, are hindered by confusion about the digital revolution. Parallel tracks of theory and study have sprung to life in various fields in response to this dislocation, and whenever they intersect, extensive competition and "poaching" takes place. This is a logical response in market-driven settings where it makes as much sense to hoard knowledge as it does to share it. Ironically, the very digital revolution that could breed increased collaboration is no match for the professional system of information hoarding that so typifies the modern business organization.

Third, the playing field is not level. The American system of professions that Abbott (1988) describes confers greater power on some and lesser power on others. Abbott defines the role of professional expertise by means of a "narrative," and it is increasingly possible to analyze both the impact of technology and the general study of organizations from the same perspective. Indeed, individuals who study the abstractions that guide the political control of "skill" and "knowledge" increase their chances of successful navigation through changing organizations.

How should librarians and other information professionals think about their role in an environment that is at once challenged by the Trojan Horse of technology but constrained by the very individual response of protecting and hoarding knowledge? The solutions to this dilemma are far from clear, and a variety of researchers are studying how organizations can respond. Those who study the workings of the conflict between shared power and hoarded power and who are able to map solutions to the issues of trust, information sharing, and skill sharing will have a substantial impact on the idea of the organization. Because of this, the traditional values of librarianship—collection, access, and counsel—may have renewed importance in the era of the continuously changing organization.

Rather than focus on the discrete study of libraries, this chapter maps parallel concepts about information, community and expertise that are at work in a variety of disciplines. First, the role of information in organizations is explored, particularly as it is understood by types of professionals. Second, the destabilizing effects of technology upon organizations are discussed, along with the increased incidence of research interest across formerly distinct disciplinary boundaries. Guiding themes and "narratives" about information in organizations are mapped and evaluated in Sections III–V, and a new narrative for individual librarians is proposed. The new narrative challenges librarians to focus on core skills during periods of organizational change and to "migrate" through increasingly fluid organizations. In the conclusion, three recommendations are offered in response to the growing surge of organizational and societal change.

II. Digital Technology and Organizations

A. Theorists and Practitioners

The rapid introduction of digital technology has created turmoil in all of the academic disciplines that are concerned with work and information. In academia, it is increasingly important to traverse disciplinary boundaries to study social and technological issues. In society at large, a new culture of continuous organizational change has become the norm, with broad implications for local, regional, and global cultures. This dynamic environment is forcing organizations, particularly business firms, to learn how to adapt quickly to new conditions. The impact of technology on librarians is but one part of the larger "story" of organizational change.

As a subspecialty of business administration, organization studies have been transition for many years, in large part because firms themselves have been constantly changing. However, the field has been well positioned to respond to the changes of the marketplace by virtue of its interdisciplinary focus. Organization studies are generally grouped into two research categories: macrophenomena and microphenomena. At the macro level, organizations may be understood as the summation of thousands of "microevents": the deeds and actions of people who are involved in an "organizing process" (Collins, 1981). The micro level of study focuses on individual behavior and has its roots in psychology (Pfeffer, 1982). Approaching organizations from these theoretical starting points has enabled the theorists to conduct empirical studies in an intellectually rigorous manner and to utilize the research techniques of related fields.

However, the impact of technological change has sparked much wider interest in organization studies. Consultants and other practitioners have been gaining influence in the study of organizations because they possess the advantage of hands-on experience. Many prominent consultants have left academia to try out ideas in the laboratory of the firm. Through practical experience, they have developed ideas about how people and technology work together, and they join forces with working managers. Broad interest in digital technology has created a lucrative publishing market for these business consultants because their applied experience enables them to respond to the needs of changing organizations more quickly than academic theorists (Hammer, 1996; Champy, 1995, 1996; Peters, 1992; Hammer and Champy, 1993).

Because organizations are changing so quickly, the dialogue between practitioners is more influential than the dialogue between theoreticians. This is a side effect of unsettled conditions in the global economy and the impact of digital technology. Moreover, digital technology enables managers to dissolve artificial, departmental boundaries that block productivity, but to do so requires new perspectives on the workplace (Levine, 1995). In essence, the business organization is being redefined by digital technology. Negroponte (1995) defines digital media as a "bitstream" of binary values that may be manipulated infinitely; the only limitations on this mutable resource are computing power and the collective imagination. The organization is being studied in a similar vein; if markets and the "microevents" of human labor can be utterly reorganized by digital technology, it follows that the organizations we work in must also become mutable (Handy, 1996b). This perspective on digital technology is causing a variety of academics and professionals to rethink the role of information in organizations.

B. The Power of Practitioner Wisdom

Digital technology has stimulated creative thinking on a broad scale. Managers, information professionals, and social scientists find that as formerly authoritative theories about organizations are reevaluated, they may advance their own hypotheses about organizations with greater certainty. The turmoil caused by continuous change in the workplace has created an intellectual environment where a variety of professionals and academics may now "diagnose" the ills and deficits of organizations and propose "treatments" that will improve them, regardless of their own native disciplines. The most influential of these new researchers will be evaluated in Sections II, III, and IV.

As managers try various strategies to stay competitive, they become more willing to engage in high-risk change processes (Hammer, 1990,1995, 1996; McNerney, 1996; Levine, 1995). Although profitability and performance are the top priorities, managers are also experimenting with ways to reconcile centralized authority with staff empowerment, which is made more possible by new technology (Institute for the Future, 1995). The tension between control and empowerment is heavily influenced by individual interactions within the firm, which range from caution (as hierarchies crumble) to excitement (as "high-tech" employees explore teamwork and collaboration)

(Schrage, 1990b). Librarians and other information specialists, along with most other types of professionals, are involved in a process of redefinition to meet the demands of continuous change.

C. "Treatment Substitution" and Organizations

1. Diagnosis and Treatment

To a large degree, organizational design is determined by the allocation of expert labor and decision making authority. However, digital technology has also shaken the stability of professions, and it has become essential to evaluate the role of expertise in light of the impact of technology. Abbott's (1988) broad analysis of the system of professions sheds considerable light on the relationship between expert labor, technology, and organizational design and offers some explanation for patterns of competition between different professions. By virtue of their expertise, professionals may "diagnose" and "treat" perceived needs and are regulated by their peers. Expert status is determined by possession of sound and irrefutable abstract knowledge, a symbolic system controlled by the profession and applied to practical problems. Professions that lose control of their system of abstract knowledge risk the loss of prestige and status (Abbott, 1988).

Digital technology creates new areas of responsibility, not only in the information professions, but also in medicine, law, and the sciences. Professions attempt to take over new areas of responsibility (such as those created by new technology) by practicing "treatment substitution": in essence, by offering a better treatment than their competitors. New types of *abstract knowledge*, such as the ability to understand how people use technology and information resources, are important sources of new professional power in organizations.

Because digital technology brings such sweeping opportunities to reorganize work, managers profit from competition among the professions. Indeed, the new credibility of nontraditional players, such as inventors, programmers, or technologically competent social scientists, is an important side benefit of digital technology (Negroponte, 1995). These individuals have embarked upon the process of treatment substitution, using new knowledge about how people and digital technology interact. This in turn sparks retaliation by established players. Flexible organizations and innovative managers try to take advantage of this ferment, which fosters cross-disciplinary solutions.

Treatment substitution holds three important lessons for the information professions. First, power, or the standing to diagnose and treat, is best maintained by the strategic preservation of abstract knowledge. Second, constant self-evaluation exposes weakness in the abstract underpinnings of professional expertise, which can invite competition. Third, digital technology offers new groups the chance to build influence and prestige, if their practitioner skills and experience give them new abstract knowledge. Because of these factors, all of the information professions are using digital technology to gain political leverage in continuously changing organizations.

2. Examples of Abstract Knowledge

To test the idea that abstract knowledge fuels professional authority, consider an example from a field of health care: acupuncture. Acupuncturists analyze "energy flows," or "Qi"; they might find a "damp wind" in the liver, or a "deficiency" in one of six distinct pulses. Treatment consists of sticking thin needles under the skin. To accept diagnosis and treatment, it is essential to accept the abstract knowledge of the profession. Clients pay for services because of the perceived value of a highly abstract knowledge system (Beinfield and Korngold, 1992).

Just as acupuncturists possess special knowledge and perform unique diagnoses and treatments, so also management researchers diagnose the organization. In doing so, researchers pursue levels of abstraction that approach the holistic, even mystical beliefs of acupuncture. For example, Charles Handy has diagnosed organizations using Greek mythology. He finds four principal organizational paradigms and designates a deity to each paradigm: Zeus, Apollo, Athena, and Dionysus (Handy, 1995, 1996b). Likewise, Abbott (1988) diagnoses the system of professions by charting individual and group development as "narratives" or "novels" of self-improvement. A highly abstract view of how people function in organizations and communities is at the crux of both Handy's and Abbott's analyses. Because these abstractions help us see how organizations (or professions) function, they challenge us to think creatively. Therefore, despite the highly abstract nature of the analysis, diagnoses and treatments such as Handy's organizational pantheon are taken seriously.

3. Imagining the Organization

If digital media can be described as mutable resources that are limited only by computing power and the collective imagination, then the ability to imagine becomes strategically important for information professionals. Organizational theorists such as Handy (1994, 1996a,b) and Pfeffer (1982) understand this; so also do sociologists (Abbott, 1988; Brown and Duguid, 1996; Murphy, 1996) and computer scientists (Negroponte, 1995). Continuous change is creating opportunities for cross-disciplinary explorations of the idea of the organization, and a growing number of critics and researchers are seizing the opportunity. Even traditional institutions such as universities and government agencies are transforming business practices with new technology, and consequently they are undergoing changes that require risk and imagination.

4. Penalties for Inaction

Digital technology is challenging all information professionals to embark upon new journeys within organizations. Reference service in corporate libraries is the best of many examples; personal relationships are built "in the field," and nurtured by access to remote resources. The emergence of new information resources such as the Internet and corporate intranets are excellent opportunities for leadership by librarians. Moreover, failure to take active steps into new areas of skill and authority carries a double penalty, because digital technology causes widespread convergence of existing tasks. Windows of opportunity for "treatment substitution" by librarians will open and close quickly; therefore complacency in continuously changing organizations is foolhardy (Yoffie, 1996).

As new opportunities for information management are created, treatment substitution increases. It is now common for publishers, libraries, or university departments to announce new publishing missions as direct consumer services, using digital libraries, or retailing techniques to bypass their former business partners. Indeed, "disintermediation," the replacement of human intermediaries with automated processes, is a concern for all of the professions (Cisler, 1996). Yet in an organizational context, the struggle for control of technology that occurs between various groups is the best indicator of the new value of information management. Davenport's work on information technology in business provides the clearest example of a manager's treatment for corporate librarianship (Davenport, 1994; Davenport and Prusak, 1993). In his article "Blow up the Corporate Library," he questions the library profession's historical success in offering information services, and his treatment is to place qualitative information management in the hands of "information guides" who would be trained in business schools.

5. Narrative For Strategic Action

Librarians, like managers, should evaluate organizations and formulate narratives for strategic action. This is a creative process which involves studying the forces driving continuous change at the macro level and imagining what an information-rich organization needs to be. Empirical data about user patterns, together with the accumulated knowledge about user needs and user research strategies that librarians gain through practice, are powerful tools for understanding productivity and relative performance (American Library Association, 1989). Narratives should be based on a broader view of organizational development than the library profession has hitherto concerned itself, precisely because digital technology invites cross-disciplinary analysis.

III. Conventional Responses to Digital Technology

Both the public and private sectors are struggling to implement practical uses for wide area networks, intranets, and the Internet. This dialogue reveals both creativity and confusion. The process of trial-and-error that managers are involved in reflects the application of proven sources of abstract knowledge to new kinds of organizational problems. The confusion is most evident in issues that involve information management from centralized hierarchies. For example, Internet end-users widely agree that when you are in cyberspace, you are "everywhere at the same time." Files and discussions run on multiple servers in an open-system environment, blurring concepts of ownership and control. However, hierarchical managers tend to covet such control. The refusal to face up to changing technology has led to the implementation of conventional business strategies in cyberspace, often with unfavorable results (Thierauf, 1995; Murphy, 1996, Institute for the Future, 1995).

Marketing on the Internet, the debate over intellectual property, and the mismatch between new technologies and old personnel practices provide evidence of technology's universal challenge and the potential for possessors of new abstract knowledge to make important contributions to business plans.

A. Marketing

Marketing on the World Wide Web has been plagued by the application of assumptions about users' willingness to conform to conventional patterns of behavior. Early marketers produced "sampler" data on the Web that was limited in scope and then charged a fee for full access. The problem was simple: consumers expected all the information to be free (Schwartz, 1996; Washburn, 1995). In essence, traditional abstract knowledge initially blocked marketers from seeing and adapting to the dispersed and libertarian culture of the Internet. In the past 2 years, marketers have improved their strategies and are currently at work on Internet marketing programs which allow users to consent to being contacted. But the early assumption that digital commerce would respond to conventional marketing strategies was a costly mistake (The Economist, 1996b). Recently, marketers have been able to borrow abstract knowledge from other fields, such as communications theory, psychology and social informatics. They have developed niche services worth 120 million dollars per year, with one billion dollars per year forecast by the year 2000. Notably, *The Wall Street Journal* has reformulated its plans to offer a Web version on a pay-for-use basis that reflects recent user patterns (Rebello, 1996; Wildstrom, 1996).

B. Intellectual Property

The concept of intellectual property is in a period of flux in the United States. In late 1995, the U.S. Department of Commerce published a "white paper" on intellectual property (also known as the "Lehman Report") (U.S. Information Infrastructure Task Force, 1995). This document has been skewered by many legal experts because of its bias toward copyright ownership, which it protects at the expense of "fair use" access to free information (The Economist, 1996a). Possessors of new symbolic knowledge such as Negroponte (1995) and Samuelson (1996) argue that new models for sharing information are needed instead of a reactive tightening of copyright laws. The lack of balance in the White Paper places the entire educational infrastructure at risk, because it trivializes the role of free access to information for scholarly purposes. The lopsided conclusions of the task force illustrate how unprepared many corporations and government agencies are to discover or recognize the advantages open-system environments and how they might improve productivity and equality for both producers and consumers. Broad debate about intellectual property has sprung to life to address the shortcomings in the copyright paradigms that are being proposed by libertarian net advocates and by traditionalists such as lawyers.

C. "Collaboration" and "Trust"

Kramer and Tyler (1996) find a curvilinear relationship between technology and trust. Management's concerns about trust are the highest when new technology is introduced, the lowest in the second stage, and then rise again in the third stage of use. An example from the information-rich profession of law is instructive. As law firms implement centralized databases of legal memoranda in order to retrieve past research and opinions, attorneys often resist sharing their work at the outset, since promotion to partnership is based on individual skill and expertise. Before attorneys will share their hard-won knowledge with the firm at large, promotion practices have to be updated in ways that reward team building while retaining the markers that identify individual talent. The only way the firm will get a central databank of legal research is by adapting its incentives; but to do so might require a major revision of the firm's personnel policies, a potentially risky step.

D. New Organizational Models for the Humanities

Abstract knowledge among humanists is producing new diagnoses and treatments to handle the flow of information within organizations. In recent years, the increased interest in the social context of technology has given birth to several new fields of inquiry, which can be described as "social informatics"

(Indiana University, 1996). It is noteworthy that some of the best analyses of the impact of technology on organizations come not from management, but from this new interdisciplinary area, which includes the humanities and the social sciences (Huwe and Schnier, 1995). The social informatics includes diverse specialists, including anthropologists, information scientists, sociologists, political scientists, and artists, yet they are all technically conversant in software and hardware contexts.

An enlightening example of the power of networking to "unseat" the conventional order may be found in the current debate about scholarly communications. The J. Paul Getty Museum's Getty Information Institute was formed to study the impact of technology on scholarship. The participants suspended preconceptions about academia in order to isolate the best responses to technology. As part of the project, Garrett (1995) explores the uncertainty of traditional roles in an era of nearly constant technological change. He argues that it is better to view scholarly communications as a continuum. Research, publication, and dissemination are studied as "zones of progressive release" upon that continuum. Instead of focusing on the known players such as professors, publishers, museums, or libraries, Garrett argues that we must study the zone of added value that each player represents and then redefine organizations to meet the needs of each player more effectively.

In effect, "many-to-many" (and, conversely, "one-to-one") communication via the Internet has challenged the status quo in academia. Tenure, peer review, and refereed journals have long been the stamps of approval for research and professional standing; yet anyone can publish on the World Wide Web. How will output be refereed in such a fluid environment? Who will collect royalties or status, and how will spurious copies be controlled in the future, particularly if data are sensitive or even vital (as in clinical medical studies)? New players such as strategically focused professional associations may emerge as independent purveyors of professional status and quality, a role now dominated by universities.

The historical underpinnings of the information professions and their future roles in organizations are increasingly volatile. Garrett's (1995) strategy of reevaluating the role of every player in this light is an instructive strategy for many other organizational theorists, who propose many treatments for organizational transformation (Banner and Gagne, 1995).

IV. Three Defining Organizational Themes

While a full review of organization studies literature would be too vast for this chapter, three themes stand out as guiding narratives that characterize how managers, social scientists, and librarians diagnose and treat continuously changing organizations. First, among managers, the "nexus of contracts" is described by Handy (1994). Second, among social scientists, the "social life" of information is being studied. Instead of viewing information as static or inanimate, social scientists study information as a lively, dynamic process. This is a narrative of discovery of how people, organizations, and information interact. Finally, among librarians, the guiding narrative is skillfulness, the mastery of information retrieval in any environment. Taken together, these defining narratives reveal how the different groups are forming new organizational strategies in continuously changing organizations. These strategies also reveal turmoil in the abstract underpinnings of each group's knowledge base, which in turn makes the struggle over information technology more pointed.

A. The "Nexus of Contracts"

Handy (1994) provides a definition of the virtual corporation as a "nexus of contracts" between individuals. People come together for discrete projects, yet view themselves as independent contractors. Handy's early awareness of the potential of a flexible workforce is followed by many other researchers who are interested in changing rigid corporations into flexible, lean firms. Practitioners counsel an increased focus on flexibility, which draws inspiration from the relationships between professional colleagues in service firms (Peters, 1992; Hammer, 1995,1996; Hammer and Champy, 1993; Davenport and Prusak, 1993). Under this narrative, twenty-first century organizations will increasingly challenge all employees to practice professional skills and be masters of their career paths (Institute for the Future, 1996). However, the nexus must be tempered by teamwork and collaboration, concepts that were popularized by Deming (1986), the father of the "total quality" movement. Deming challenges managers to balance the idea that the workforce is a flexible commodity with the competing idea that it is vital resource, which should be empowered and nurtured (Gitlow and Gitlow, 1987). The strategies managers are exploring to respond to this confused but exciting environment are frequently referred to as "new work practices" (Levine, 1995; Ichniowski, *et al.*, 1996).

Often accused of "faddishness," management researchers nonetheless are operating during a period of profound opportunity. Large-scale transformations of corporate structure are increasingly commonplace in the United States; high-stakes "reengineering" projects can spur new bestsellers even when the theory behind the program must undergo major revision and apologia (Hammer, 1995, 1996; White, 1996). To help firms survive, Senge (1990) counsels managers to make use of technology, social science, and cultural studies in order to form "learning organizations."

Rosow and Hickey (1995) argue that change is not separable from the ongoing work of the organization and that it is an open-ended process. More importantly, they challenge managers to live by the mandates they set for employees. In doing so they also challenge shareholders to reevaluate their social contract with employees, opening a debate about the proper balance of shareholder profits and wages.

It is difficult for management to frame the "nexus of contracts" in structures that also support trust and teamwork and provide an acceptable level of employment security (Levine, 1995; Ichniowski *et al.*, 1996). The abstract goal of "the nexus of contracts" is to force managers to address the outdated paradigm of the centrally controlled corporation and, through experimentation, find a new balance between individual responsibility and authority (Institute for the Future, 1995). Information professionals find themselves reacting to these strategies because management can define the goals of information resources management within the larger goals of the firm. Consequently, the nexus of contracts has become a durable narrative for management, which ultimately receives its authority to define the organization from shareholders.

B. The "Social Life of Documents"

While management researchers focus on ways to harness teamwork and build nonhierarchical models, social scientists are studying the social context of technology. By evaluating human interaction with technology, social scientists have successfully gained a new area of authority as design critics.

John Seely Brown (1991) was involved in work on graphical user interfaces during the Seventies and has recently been studying the meaning and structure of information itself (Brown and Duguid, 1996). Instead of viewing information as a series of numeric quantities or static verbiage, he argues that documents, whether medieval manuscripts, books, or computer files, are dynamic containers of information about people and their social contexts. They are changed by each author, perhaps as palimpsests or through dog-eared pages, margin notes, graffiti, and so on. By casting the document as a receptacle for lively information, Brown is challenging designers of computers and organizations to treat their design media more creatively. Wilensky (1996), himself a computer scientist, has collaborated with social scientists to build digital libraries. He has defined parameters for multivalent documents: multilayered, multidimensional, interactive computer files, which combine bibliographic tools and content.

Bonnie Nardi, an anthropologist and Fellow with Apple Computer's Advanced Research Group, has studied "virtual agents," software code that can automate the retrieval of information and save time for the user (Nardi and O'Day, 1996). While conducting field work in corporate libraries, Nardi discovered that reference is a highly nuanced and subtle communications strategy. Given the richness of communication in reference, she argues that virtual agents should be only one part of a "diverse, information ecology." The information ecology would allow people to weave reference, automated assistance, databases, and print media into a single context.

Schrage (1990a,b) and Negroponte (1995) both challenge computer designers to focus on human interaction. Both support Nardi's theories about the qualitative differences between intelligent agents and human interaction. Schrage argues that computers should be technologies of collaboration, while Negroponte focuses on the mutability of digital technology and the opportunities it presents to reevaluate not only organizational structure and human–machine interactions, but just about everything.

William J. Mitchell (1995), Dean of Architecture at MIT, extends the mutability theory of digital media by writing an entire book about the architecture of virtual reality. Daring and entertaining, the book poses an interesting question: how will architects design for a future where structures, and the events that occur within them, are digital? As computing becomes "ubiquitous," insinuated into everyday objects, there will be related impacts on housing, work, and our concepts of space. Such speculation might be dismissed as "mere philosophy" instead of rigorous scholarship but for the demonstrated mutability of digital media, which demands abstract descriptions of this sort.

But testing the limits of imagination brings its own dilemmas. Ober (1995) finds that the metaphors we use to describe digital media are being stretched past understandable contexts, making the teaching of multimedia more challenging. The pursuit of meaningful metaphors opens the door to linguistic evaluation of digital media, and the linguistics suggest the importance of understanding cognitive development as we interact with technology.

New social science research about information and organizations demonstrates the importance of interdisciplinary research. Specialists simply must consult with one another to understand the effects of new technology. Moreover, social science research shines a spotlight on the wavering boundaries of traditional disciplines. Negroponte was originally a computer scientist specializing in artificial intelligence; Nardi is an anthropologist who also studies computers. Although he is a computer scientist, Negroponte has gained standing to speak about organizations, and as an anthropologist, Nardi has gained standing to speak about libraries and software. Ultimately, all of these researchers need to consult one another to be able to make sense in their own fields and in broader social contexts.

The defining theme for social science research about information is a narrative of discovery. Basically, social scientists are concerned with what people are "really doing" with information.

C. Librarians and "Skillfulness"

Abbott (1988), in describing the history of the library profession, says that librarians suffered little or no competition from other professions until recently. The early goals of the profession were based on a humanistic tradition of "improvement," which included literacy advocacy and knowledge classification. Berring sees an early commitment to the distribution of skill rather than the hoarding of expertise through licensure and private practice (Berring 1995). But in the era of the Internet, where, as Bill Gates put it, "content is king" (Lewis, 1995), it seems that everyone is competing with librarians to manage information. Hawley (1995) speculates that in the future, library-based selection and organization of information might become a "cottage industry," since everyone will be able to do this locally.

Academics librarians such as Walt Crawford, and Michael Gorman (1995) Walt Crawford, Michael Gorman (1995) and Robert C. Berring (1995) reply that there are several roles that librarians should continue to play, chief of which are collection, access, and preservation of the cultural record. Moreover, even managers themselves concede that one outcome of "scientific management" (Taylor, 1915) has been the balkanization of information throughout the organization in separate departments (Hammer, 1990; McFarlan and McKenney, 1983; McFarlan, *et al.*, 1983; McKinnon and Bruns, 1992). Gorman is a strong advocate of the universal importance and applicability of library-based information management techniques, while Berring (1995) considers the library profession's prospects by evaluating the threats posed by new competition. He groups librarians' responses to the competition into three camps: conservative, reformist, and radical. The conservatives would shun digital technology and focus on print resources, while reformers would make a compromise with the digital revolution. The radicals turn their backs on history and march boldly into a future without impediment. All three options are problematic in Berring's opinion, who suggests that the last, best chance for librarians lies in partnerships with information producers, where they might be able to carve out a niche as experts in end user requirements. Berring summarizes this role as "information filtering": a combination of "selective dissemination of information" techniques and long-term strategies for preservation.

In the workplace, library practitioners provide a snapshot of skillfulness in action and the rewards it can bring. At the 87th Annual Conference of the Special Libraries Association in June, 1996, several corporate librarians lectured on the new roles they have assumed in firms. One of these, Rebekah Anderson of 3M Corporation, explained how library services were not only defining several key information processes throughout the firm, but were also fully integrated into highly important roles, such as disaster response teams.

Other examples included close partnerships between the strategic planning department and the library at Digital Equipment Corporation and organization-wide information management by the library at MIT's Lincoln Laboratory (Williamson, *et al.*, 1996).

There were three common features to all of the examples. First, the success enjoyed was attributable to good individual leadership and promotional skills. Second, each individual viewed the firm as a "diverse, information ecology" and used this awareness to be proactive beyond the library. In essence, they made their skill understandable to nonlibrary professionals by taking library skills beyond their own domain. Third, and most important, they did not retreat from the information counseling role of the librarian. Instead, they understood that as technology opens new platforms for group collaboration, reference and related interpersonal interactions will become much more important.

Stories like these do not often appear beyond the discrete domain of library literature, as special librarians tend to interact mainly within the library profession. But if copying is the highest compliment one can be paid, a close review of Davenport's work reveals an excellent example of treatment substitution (Davenport, 1994; Davenport and Prusak, 1993). Davenport argues that information is so vast that corporations must develop "information guides" to meet the challenge. The new employee is really a reference librarian with another name, but the new role transfers information counseling away from librarians and into business administration.

In the present era of continuous organizational change, the defining theme of librarianship is skillfulness. As competitors attempt to take charge of information management, librarians respond that the interlopers lack a historical perspective on both user needs and the societal mission of libraries (Crawford and Gorman, 1995). Indeed, as large scale digital library research is conducted, new, interdisciplinary research groups find themselves struggling over definitions of what information is and how to structure access, yet they miss library literature's treatments entirely (Jacobson, 1995). This struggle to redefine information reopens opportunity for the historic skill holders, if they can convey the importance of their skill.

The theme of skillfulness is also employed in the revised mission statements of library schools. At the University of California at Berkeley, the recently formed School of Information Management and Systems defines its prospective students as follows:

> Information managers must be familiar with the technology used to store, organize and retrieve information in business, government, library and academic settings. However, technical expertise alone is not sufficient for success; graduates will be expected to only to

manage technology, but to manage information and people as well, and they need to acquire the necessary skills to do this effectively.

(*University of California, 1994*)

V. Toward an Organizational Narrative

Most if not all of the theories that were explored in Sections II, III, and IV are well-reasoned attempts to make sense of the idea of the organization and its community of members. Embedded within these theories (unconsciously, in some cases) is the idea of the library as a service, storehouse, or lively community where knowledge is exchanged. But all these theories about work and organization take place within a larger organizational narrative that guides our expectations from firms.

In order to conceptualize, diagnose, and treat the organizational dislocation caused by digital technology, it is necessary to develop an organizational narrative, or "story," of development for the organization. Abbott (1988) uses this hypothesis to describe how the system of professions guides individuals in their careers; he calls this story a "novel of self-improvement." Likewise, many researchers struggle with the abstract idea of the organization and offer interesting models for conception. The Institute for the Future (1995) employs metaphors and uses them to define six types of twenty-first century organizations; but the metaphorical models (ranging from "hyper-focused" to "self-generating") operate in a continuously changing environment, and they concede that the metaphors are likely to mutate over time.

A "story," or narrative, for the goals of the organization could inform and guide individuals within the constantly changing workplace in much the same way that Abbott's novel of self-improvement provides a map for individual professional development. However, the level of abstraction required to develop such a hypothesis is hazardous, particularly for practitioners who would prefer to focus on concrete strategies. Moreover, the application of single narrative concepts to organizations in general invites charges of reductionism and determinism, as Pfeffer points out about organization studies in general (Pfeffer, 1982, Institute for the Future, 1995).

But the risks of reductionism have not stopped an array of respectable scholars from exploring new and intellectually provocative approaches to the "story" of organizations, as Negroponte's (1995) study of digital media and Mitchell's (1995) analysis of architecture demonstrate. The mutability of digital media *requires* abstract thinking and a wide, interdisciplinary focus to be understood at all. Abstraction and metaphor offer the only available means of understanding a binary stream of zeroes and ones as "virtual reality," and Ober (1995) has argued that the metaphors are losing ground.

Nonetheless, librarians and other information professionals need to navigate through organizations in an era of turmoil. It is essential for them to revise and update their abstract knowledge about information and organizations in order to succeed on this journey. The best place to start is with a sense of the narrative that is driving organizational design. In order to challenge creative thinking about libraries and the idea of the organization, a guiding definition of the organization is proposed in Section V,A. This guiding definition can be described as "Kaizen," or "continuous improvement."

A. "Kaizen"

Kaizen is the Japanese term Deming (1986) adopted to define the goals of the total quality movement. In Section V,B, librarians are challenged to form strategies that make full use of Kaizen as a basis for strategic action within continuously changing organizations. Recognition of Kaizen enables librarians to use the current turmoil in management and social sciences research to their advantage; by specifically tailoring library-based information skills to harness the rhetorical energy of "continuous improvement," librarians can recast their core skills to build productivity in knowledge-based firms. Kaizen also allows librarians to reinvigorate their historical mission of "improvement" and to see this historical goal as an important "microevent" within organizations (Crawford and Gorman, 1995).

Kaizen is the organization-wide commitment to continuous improvement in all aspects of work. Although Kaizen usually refers to industrial techniques, "reengineering" and other consulting strategies use the concept more generally (Hammer, 1990, 1995, 1996). As a defining narrative for the organization, Kaizen brings the elements of continuous improvement into focus. These range from entrepreneurial activity, such as venture capitalism, to strategic programs such as "downsizing" for the sake of productivity gains. Kaizen can be used to justify any number of management strategies because it is difficult to object to continuous improvement on any grounds. Therefore draconian strategies such as downsizing, restructuring, revamping political parties, or reorganizing university curricula all invoke the Kaizen paradigm to build support at all levels within organizations. In this regard, Kaizen operates as a guiding narrative that focuses energy and consensus. In continuously changing organizations, consultants argue that employees will become "process managers," which for many people, is a vastly different way to work. To make this new reality more palatable, they invoke Kaizen as an incentive: in order to help the firm survive, reticent employees are asked to believe in the change program for the sake of continuous improvement, despite the risks to their job security.

Indeed, the Kaizen narrative is employed frequently as a rhetorical call to unity and action. For example, it is now widely agreed that government should be "reinvented," and institutions in general should make maximum use of technology to improve productivity and reduce costs (Gore, 1995; Carroll, 1995). But as with most forms of rhetoric, whether the goal is actually achieved matters less than the successful galvanization of public opinion, which allows leaders to follow a variety of goals as they see fit (Carroll, 1995). Likewise, Kaizen may be used not only as a rhetorical tool by managers, but also by professionals to gain power within organizations. In short, "continuous improvement" can be used to build mass organizational consensus, and it can also be used to advance into new roles and to obtain new areas of professional authority.

The special librarians described in Section IV employed the Kaizen narrative for their own advantage by demonstrating that library skill was not only good but essential to the continuous improvement of the firm. Similarly, Negroponte (1995), Schrage (1990a,b), and Davenport (1994) are shaping the idea of the organization by invoking the mandate for continuous improvement by all possible means. When continuous improvement is invoked to justify treatment substitutions such as laying off librarians and hiring "information guides," it carries powerful rhetorical leverage that is based on the widely accepted belief that continuous improvement is a good thing. It diminishes the effectiveness of arguments against the move and taps a powerful rhetorical basis for seizing the abstract knowledge bases of specific professions. However, the same strategy can be employed in favor of libraries, and the turmoil within organization studies that is described in Sections II, III, and IV invite the attempt.

Rather than endlessly reevaluating their problems and historical burdens, librarians should begin to think about their roles within organizations with Kaizen in mind. The challenge that librarians must confront comes not from some deficit in their skills, which outsiders such as Bonnie Nardi praise and visionaries such as Davenport covet. Neither does the challenge lie in their mission, which is a prized role that many players are struggling to dominate (Nardi and O'Day, 1996; Davenport, 1994). Instead, their problem lies in failing to practice treatment substitution the process Abbott (1988) describes to demonstrate competition among professions. Kaizen provides librarians with a narrative framework for taking an active role in shaping organizations. By invoking Kaizen in support of library services they could practice treatment substitution, and take charge of the electronic domains that are opening. At the very least, thinking about *organizations themselves* as mutable agents in the bitstream of technology challenges librarians to *migrate* along with the changing organization, instead of resisting the forces of change. While Berring

(1995) would characterize such a strategy as "radical," migration into new roles is also pragmatic because organizations will continue to change.

B. Strategies for Librarians

The link between an abstract discussion of narratives that guide the idea of the organization and actual professional practice is important. The three specific recommendations that follow give substantive directions for action that are informed by the review of the organization and the professions in Sections II, III, and IV.

1. Migrating with Skillfulness

Reference, or "information counsel" is an essential skill that should not be allowed to disappear (Huwe, 1993, 1996). Collection management and access are also essential. The markets for these skills are not diminishing, they are growing. However, they are growing in new locations such as virtual communities, digital libraries, Internet search engines, and new information-rich departments within firms (James-Catalano, 1996). Librarians should review the opportunities presented by technologies of collaboration and by digital libraries and take the initiative in forming partnerships with the designers (Huwe, 1993). They should also form strategic partnerships with information producers to influence system design (Berring, 1995).

2. Virtual Communities and Nongovernmental Organizations

Rheingold (1993) explores the idea of community as the natural appearance of new species taking niches in an ecosystem. In his particular example, the ecosystem is cyberspace, where individuals are free (for the present) to form the kinds of communities they wish. Such new communities provide a natural place for skillful information counselors (H. Rheingold, personal communication).

Another interesting model is being pioneered in the developing world. "Nongovernmental organizations" (NGOs) are important service providers in developing countries. They operate with quasiofficial status and provide an "upward" bias for action on behalf of their members (Ndegwa, 1994; Lingscheid, 1995; Clark, 1995). In developing countries, NGOs provide services and community-building spirit that governments either cannot provide or choose to avoid. This kind of organization should lend itself very effectively to virtual communities, many of which already exist outside of national or governmental boundaries. In more affluent societies, the wealth and infrastructure already exist to integrate the best of community involvement, information discovery and management, and self-determination in cyberspace, but the NGO model goes largely undiscovered. Library skill has a place in the NGO, whether in the developing world or in the United States. The NGO model provides a new opportunity for librarians to assume upward leadership and participate in communities where skillfulness in information management could be recognized and valued.

3. Reorganize Professional Associations

Librarians should consider revamping their professional associations. The argument that technology will replace or automate mediated human interaction with knowledge resources is neither accurate nor helpful to end users. Professional literature now validates the study of the social impact of computing, and the working culture of reference holds a key to productivity that few nonlibrarians understand clearly. The best way to participate in these exciting developments is to join the professional discussions of the groups that control the dialogue.The logical targets are management and computer science. As members, librarians could seek leadership in these associations and host programs at annual meetings. However, they might need to curtail such efforts in their "home" associations, which could atrophy as a result.

Currently, it is common for librarians to belong to five or more national associations, including the American Library Association, the Special Libraries Association, the American Association for Information Science, and so on. The total dues burden for membership in so many groups is substantial. Abbott (1988) finds that associations and journals change only when their mission changes. At present, it appears that what librarians lack most is a voice that is heard outside their own field. Nardi and O'Day (1996) confirm this as spectators of the high-quality work performed in libraries; indeed, their strongest recommendation to librarians is to promote themselves outside their native domain. If library associations are not able to capture the imagination of the populace, then librarians should be willing to move into associations which can do so.

Alternatively, library professional associations might consider recruiting new members who are information professionals, but who do not possess the MLS degree. Such a move would swell membership ranks and open debate about libraries in a larger context. Many citizens care deeply about libraries, yet they are largely left out of professional dialogue about the future of the profession. It is not unusual for large associations to hire publicists to make sure that the goals of the group are well known; perhaps efforts of this sort would boost the profession through expansion.

VI. Conclusion

The idea of the organization is formed collectively by society, and may be understood as a "story" or narrative about what we do in community with one another. The role of expertise is structured by system of professions, which allocates skill within organizations. Information technology is disintegrating the boundaries between professional skill and changing organizations in dynamic ways. The vacuum created by wavering professional boundaries and the unraveling of formerly solid abstract knowledge bases within professions has had an especially pronounced impact on the information professions and has accelerated the rate of competition between different information professionals. This new vacuum has also prompted forays by other professionals into the information field. These events bring crisis and opportunity not only for librarians, but for the entire professional class.

Organizations and the professions have related narratives. While professionals embark upon story of professional development (Abbott, 1988), organizations follow the story of "Kaizen," or *continuous improvement.* These forces are interpreted in a variety of ways by management researchers, social scientists, and information professionals. As information becomes digital and more easily manipulated, the forces of change accelerate further and call into question not only the role of librarians, but of human labor generally and the structures that manage it.

Within this dynamic environment, the librarian's specific professional narrative is undergoing change. Librarians may no longer safely identify themselves solely with the *library as a site or collection;* it is becoming more necessary to identify with sets of *librarian skills.* As skill possessors, librarians can migrate to open spaces within organizations (such as new types of information management positions) and to entirely new organizations such as virtual communities or nongovernmental organizations. Therefore a new narrative, based on skillfulness and migration, offers librarians an umbrella strategy to follow in an era of continuous organizational change. However, migration does not connote abandonment of core values, but instead, the embracing of new territory. Since both technology and the idea of the organization will continue to change, migration offers a durable basis for retaining the abstract underpinnings of the library profession and the standing to speak to the information needs of people.

Acknowledgments

The author wishes to thank UC Berkeley Professors Clair Brown, Jim Lincoln, and David I. Levine for their support and inspiration; Dean Hal Varian, School of Information Management and Systems, UC Berkeley; Peter Lyman, University Librarian, UC Berkeley; Bob Berring, Law Librarian and Professor of Law, Boalt Hall, UC Berkeley; authors Michael Schrage and Howard Rheingold for their insightful comments; and Janice Kimball, for her library research.

References

Abbott, A. (1988). *The System of Professions: An Essay on the Division of Expert Labor.* University of Chicago, Chicago.

American Library Association (1989). *Presidential Committee on Information Literacy,* Final Report. ALA, Chicago.

Banner, T. K., and Gagne, T. E. (1995). *Designing Effective Organizations: Traditional and Transformational Views.* Sage, Thousand Oaks, CA.

Beinfield, H. and Korngold, E. (1992). *Between Heaven and Earth: A Guide to Chinese Medicine.* Ballantine, New York.

Berring, R. C. (1995). Future librarians. In *Future Libraries* (R. Bloch and C. Hesse, eds.). University of California Press, Berkeley.

Brown, J. S. (1991). Research that reinvents the corporation. *Harvard Buisness Review* **69,** 102–112.

Brown, J. S., and Duguid, P. (1996). The social life of documents. *First Monday* **1.** Available: http://www.firstmonday.dk.

Carroll, J. D. (1995). The rhetoric of reform and political reality in the National Performance Review. *Public Administration Review* **55,** 302–312.

Champy, J. (1995). *Reengineering Management : The Mandate for New Leadership.* HarperBusiness, New York.

Champy, J. (1996). *Fast Forward : The Best Ideas on Managing Business Change.* Harvard Business School Press, Boston.

Cisler, S. (1996). Weatherproofing a great, good place. *American Libraries* **27,** 42–46.

Clark, A. M. (1995). Non-governmental organizations and their influence on international society. *Journal of International Affairs* **48,** 507–525.

Collins, R. (1981). On the microfoundations of macrosociology. *American Journal of Sociology* **86,** 984–1014.

Crawford, W., and Gorman, M. (1995). *Future Libraries, Dreams, Madness and Reality.* American Library Assocation, Chicago.

Davenport, T. H. (1994). Saving IT's soul: Human-centered information management. *Harvard Business Review* **72,** 119–131.

Davenport, T. H., and Prusak, L. (1993). Blow up the corporate library. *International Journal of Information Management* **13.** 403–412.

Deming, W. E. (1986). *Out of the Crisis: Quality, Productivity and Competitive Position.* Cambridge University Press, Cambridge, UK.

The Economist (1996a). The property of the mind. *The Economist* **340,** 57–59.

The Economist (1996b). Pricing the net. *The Economist* **341,** 23–30.

Garrett, J. (1995). *New Economic and Social Mechanisms to Encourage Access.* Getty Information Institute. Available: http://www.ahip.getty.edu.

Gitlow, H. S., and Gitlow, S. J. (1987). *The Deming Guide to Quality and Competitive Position.* Prentice-Hall, Englewood Cliffs, NJ.

Gore, A. (1995). *Common Sense Government: Works Better and Costs Less,* Third report of the National Performance Review. U.S. Government Printing Office, Washington, DC.

Hammer, M. (1990). Reengineering: Don't automate, obliterate. *Harvard Business Review* **68,** 104–112.

Hammer, M. (1995). *The Reengineering Revolution: A Handbook.* HarperBusiness, New York.

Hammer, M. (1996). *Beyond Reengineering: How the Process-Centered Organization is Changing Our Work and Lives.* HarperBusiness, New York.

Hammer, M., and Champy, J. (1993). *Reengineering the Corporation: A Manifesto for Business Revolution.* HarperBusiness, New York.

Handy, C. (1994). *The Age of Paradox.* Harvard Business School Press, Boston.

Handy, C. (1995). *Gods of Management: The Changing Work of Organizations.* Oxford University Press, New York.

Handy, C. (1996a). *Beyond Uncertainty: The Changing Worlds of Organizations.* Harvard Business School Press, Boston.

Handy, C. (1996b). On the future of work and an end to the "century of the organization." *Organizational Dynamics* 25, 15-26.

Hawley, J. (1995). Blown to bits: Libraries in the next millennium. *FID News Bulletin* **45,** 110–115.

Huwe, T. K. (1993). Information specialists and the cooperative workplace: Challenges and opportunities. In *Advances in Librarianship* (I. Godden, ed.), Vol. 17, pp. 2–31. Academic Press, San Diego, CA.

Huwe, T. K. (1996). Knowledge transfer in cyberspace: Organizational challenges. *FID News Bulletin* **46,** 55–62.

Huwe, T. K., and Schnier, C. L. (1995). The humanistic potential of multimedia: Two conclusions. *FID News Bulletin* **45,** 104–109.

Ichniowski, C., Kochan, T. A., Levine, D., Olson, C., and Strauss, G. (1996). What works at work. *Industrial Relations* **35,** 299.

Indiana University (1996). Center for Social Informatics Mission Statement. Available: http://www-slis.indiana.edu/CSI.

Institute for the Future (1995). *Twenty-First century Organizations: Reconciling Control and Empowerment.* Institute for the Future, Menlo Park, CA.

Jacobson, R. L. (1995). Researchers temper their ambitions for digital libraries. *Chronicle of Higher Education* **42,** A19.

James-Catalano, C. N. (1996). Look to the librarians. *Internet World* **7,** 28.

Kleiner, A. (1995). The battle for the soul of corporate America. *Wired* **3.08,** 120.

Koenig, M. (1988). The transfer of library skills to nonlibrary contexts. In *Advances in Librarianship* (I. Godden, ed.) Vol. 15, pp. 1–27. Academic Press, San Diego, CA.

Kramer, R. M., and Tyler, T. R. (1996). *Trust in Organizations: Frontiers of Theory and Research.* Sage Publications, Thousand Oaks, CA.

Levine, D. I. (1995). *Reinventing the Workplace: How Business and Employees Can Both Win.* Brookings Institution, Washington, DC.

Lewis, P. H (1995). Microsoft says it's going after Internet market. *New York Times* **145** (Friday, December 8), C1.

Lingscheid, R. (1995). From consultation to participation: Non-governmental organizations and the United Nations. *Ecumenical Review.* **47,** 307.

McFarlan, F. W., and McKenney, J. L. (1983). The information archipelago—plotting a course. *Harvard Business Review* **60,** 109–119.

McFarlan, F. W., McKenney, J. L., and Pyburn, P. (1983). The information achipelago—maps and bridges. *Harvard Business Review* **61,** 145–156.

McKinnon, S., and Bruns, W. J., Jr. (1992). *The Information Mosaic: How Managers Get the Information They Really Need.* Harvard Business School Press, Boston.

McNerney, D. J. (1996). HR practices: HR adapts to continuous restructuring. *HR Focus* **73,** 1.

Mitchell, W. J. (1995). *City of Bits : Space, Place, and the Infobahn.* MIT Press, Cambridge, MA.

Murphy, S. (1996). Corporate metamorphosis: The effects of the new media. *First Monday* 2. Available: http://www.firstmonday.uk.

Nardi, B. A., and O'Day, V. (1996). Intelligent agents: What we learned at the library. *Libri* **46,** 15–45.

Ndegwa, S. N (1994). Civil society and political change in Africa: The case of non-governmental organizations in Kenya. *International Journal of Comparative Sociology* **35,** 19.

Negroponte, N. (1995). *Being Digital.* Random House, New York.

Ober, J. (1995). Challenges in teaching and learning multimedia. *FID News Bulletin* **45,** 116–120.

Peters, T. (1992). *Liberation Management.* Alfred A. Knopf, New York.

Pfeffer, J. (1982). *Organizations and Organization Theory.* Pitman, Boston.

Rebello, K. (1996). "Who's making money on the net. *BusinessWeek* **3494,** 104–111.

Rheingold, H. (1993). *The Virtual Community : Homesteading on the Electronic Frontier.* Addison-Wesley, Reading, MA.

Rosow, J., and Hickey, J. (1995). *Strategic Partners for High Performance. Part III: How Change Agents Transform the Enterprise.* Work in America Institute, Scarsdale, NY.

Samuelson, P. (1996). The copyright grab. *Wired* **4.01,** 134–138.

Schrage, M. (1990a). The healing power of high tech. *Los Angeles Times* **109,** (November 18), D9.

Schrage, M. (1990b). *Shared Minds: The Emerging Technologies of Collaboration.* Random House, New York.

Schwartz, E., I (1996). Advertising webonomics 101. *Wired* **4.02,** 74.

Senge, P. M. (1990). *The Fifth Discipline: The Art and Practice of the Learning Organization.* Doubleday/Currency, New York.

Taylor, F. (1915). *The Principles of Scientific Management.* Harper & Row, New York.

Thierauf, R. J. (1995). *Virtual Reality Systems for Business.* Quorum, Westport, CT.

U. S. Information Infrastructure Task Force (1995). Report of the Working Group in Intellectual Property Rights. U. S. Department of Commerce, Washington, D. C. Available: http://www.iitf.gov.

University of California (1994). *Mission Statement.* University of California, School of Information Management and Systems, Berkeley. Available: http://www.sims berkeley.edu.

Washburn, B. (1995). Who's making money on the net. *Internet World* **6,** 30–31.

White, J. B. (1996). Re-engineering gurus take steps to remodel their stalling vehicles. *The Wall Street Journal* **135,** (November 26), A1.

Wildstrom, S. L. (1996). VCRs for the web. *BusinessWeek* **3490,** 14.

Wilensky, R. (1996). Toward work-centered digital information services. *Computer*, May. Available: http://www.computer.org:80/pubs/computer/dli/r50037/r50037.htm.

Williamson, C., Anderson, R., Katayama, J., and Hornbach, K. (1996). Revolutionary roles: Information professionals on corporate project teams. Paper presented at the 87th Annual Conference of the Special Libraries Association, Boston.

Yoffie, D. B. (1996). Competing in the age of digital convergence. *California Management Review* **38,** 31–53.

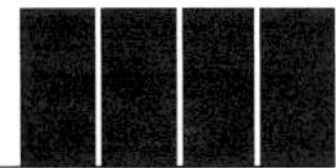

Virtual Universities and their Libraries

A Comparison of Australian and North American Experiences

Margaret Small
University of New England
Armidale 2351, Australia

In recent years a new style of university has emerged: the virtual university. This chapter considers whether virtual universities are simply the most recent development in distance education or an entirely new way of teaching at the tertiary level. Australian and North American experiences are drawn upon and the role which libraries are playing and should play within virtual universities is examined.

I. What is a Virtual University?

Many of these new universities are indistinguishable from mainstream distance teaching institutions; different only in that some use electronic means to deliver material to or to interact with students. Are these virtual universities or are they simply exploiting the next important development in communications technology? Among them, however, are some which are radically different organizationally and in their approach to learning, and some of these interact electronically with their students. Are these virtual universities?

The word "virtual" has been adopted by the computer industry; for example, the term "virtual reality" refers to an environment or object simulated by computer hard- and software in such a way that the viewer experiences the environment or object as though it were real (Nader, 1995). While virtual reality technology could be used to simulate the experience of attending lectures, using a library, and spending time in a student common room, practically speaking this is some way into the future. Rather than advocating the use of virtual reality techniques in this sense, Tiffin and Rajasingham (1995) argue that computing, radio, television, and teleconferencing are merging in virtual learning institutions. The convergence of these technologies

0065-2830/97 $25.00

will allow learners to interact with each other and with course facilitators to put together courses tailored for their specific needs and build on their existing skills and knowledge from a place and at a time of their choosing. Learners will in effect be at the center of a web of learning and support networks. Learners could access such networks through multimedia workstations in their homes, in communities, and within existing universities. These universities could in the future move away from direct teaching and become course developers and providers for virtual universities while maintaining and developing a focus on research activities (Hutchison, 1996).

The increasing availability of the Internet in the general community and a growing enthusiasm for its use have fostered an explosion of interest in delivering education electronically, especially since the development of the World Wide Web. This is, however, the exploitation of the latest new technology—the real attraction of virtual learning institutions is in the economics of not having to maintain physical facilities coupled with the prospect of being able to offer educational opportunities in ways which more closely match the needs of learners in the late twentieth century. Universities are coming to accept that it may be possible to deliver education successfully without the infrastructure which is such a feature of mainstream universities today: laboratories, libraries, student residences, health services, sporting facilities, lecture theatres, shops, and cafeterias. Most significant is the acceptance that tenured academic staff may not be needed if courses can be brought in from elsewhere or developed by a project team and taught by a contracted staff. Such a change challenges in a very fundamental way the traditional view of universities which have been seen as communities of scholars for whom peer support and interaction are essential (Gilbert, 1995). It has always been assumed that the familiar organizational pattern of academic faculties, schools, and departments is the basis for the development and teaching of integrated programs of study. The examples of the National Technological University in the United States and its Australian counterpart, Engineering Education Australia (to name only two nontraditional organisations), which draw courses from a large number of different institutions to form programs of study demonstrate that this pattern of organization is not essential.

II. Virtual Universities in Australia

A. Correspondence Schools

Distance education is well established in Australia as a legitimate educational mode at all levels from kindergarten to doctorate level. The eminent Australian historian Geoffrey Blainey said that “distance is as characteristic of

Australia as mountains are of Switzerland" (1966, p. x) to emphasize the impact which Australia's physical geography has had on its social, political and economic development. Despite having a landmass equal to that of continental United States, Australia has a population of only around 18 million, of whom the overwhelming majority live on the eastern coastal fringe. In the interior of the country (the "Outback"), the population is so sparse that many children live too far from the nearest school to allow attendance. Instead, correspondence schools have been educating Outback children since 1916.

From 1951 a peculiarly Australian invention, the Traeger transceiver set (also affectionately known as the pedal radio), added an interactive element to this otherwise isolating schooling. The pedal radio had been developed earlier for the Royal Flying Doctor Service, another uniquely Australian institution which provided emergency medical services by light aeroplane. Since many remote areas did not have any form of electricity, the pedal radio, for which the caller generated enough power to allow communication by a pedaling device, made it possible for Outback people to call for medical assistance. The Schools of the Air used the Royal Flying Doctor Service network for "classes" of children, widely separated geographically, to interact with each other and with their teachers (Ashton, 1971).

The pedal radio has now been superseded by two-way radio, satellite telephone services, audiographics, desktop videoconferencing, and email, but it did set the standard for the use of innovative communication technologies in distance education in Australia.

2. Distance Teaching Universities and Their Libraries

With such a tradition of distance teaching, it was only natural that tertiary education should also be offered at a distance. The first university in the field, the University of Queensland, which began teaching off-campus in 1911, actually pre-dates the establishment of correspondence schools. Initially off- and on-campus teaching were quite separate (the first Director of Correspondence Studies, T.C. Jones, attended lectures, made notes, and posted copies of his notes to off-campus students), and this separation continued to some extent until relatively recently. In line with this model, a separate library, the Thatcher Library, was established in 1948 to service the needs of off-campus students (Small, 1978).

It was almost half a century before the second distance teaching university in Australia entered the field. The University of New England was founded in 1954 with the mission to teach both on- and off-campus. As the University was located in a small country city, well away from major centres of population, it was feared that it would be impossible to attract sufficient numbers of on-campus students for the new institution to be viable, hence its interest in off-campus teaching. Initially most off-campus students were country school teachers seeking to upgrade their qualifications. Distance education at the University of New England has been characterized by the integration of off- and on-campus teaching and the importance given to personal contact between academic staff and students through attendance at compulsory residential schools, usually 4 days long and held in Armidale (Small, 1978).

The library service, however, was not integrated until the late 1960s. Because of the then-inadequate and slow postal service in Australia, the University initially entered into a contract with the State Library of New South Wales, which already had a country lending service using the railways as the delivery mechanism. The University assumed responsibility for providing a library service in 1971, although the collection remained separate from that servicing on-campus students until 1981 when the two were merged (Maticka, 1992).

The University's practice of requiring students to attend residential schools has provided the opportunity for off-campus students to make use of the University Library in person, a rare occurrence for such students. It also affords the Library the opportunity to provide face-to-face reader education programs for these students. At other times of the year students are able to request book loans, photocopies, and subject searches by mail, fax, and telephone. Students with appropriate equipment are able to access the Library's on-line catalog and to search a number of electronic databases. These services are typical of those provided by distance teaching universities in Australia.

In the 35 years following the establishment of the University of New England, many more universities and colleges of advanced education instituted off-campus programs. During the 1960s and 1970s a number of teacher training colleges, many in regional areas, were transformed into multidisciplinary colleges of advanced education. As with the University of New England, many of these colleges turned to off-campus teaching to boost student numbers.

By 1988, there were 72 institutions teaching at the tertiary level, 21 of which had enrollments of less than 2000 full-time student equivalents. It was clear to the Australian government (which funds tertiary education) that rationalization was in order. A government White Paper (Dawkins 1988) proposed reducing the number of tertiary institutions and the number which would be funded to teach off-campus courses. By 1992 all colleges of advanced education had been transformed into universities and/or had amalgamated with existing universities in total and the number of tertiary institutions had been halved. Eight had been designated as Distance Education Centres (DECs) which were intended to be the principal providers of distance education nationally (Lim, 1992).

The plan to confine off-campus teaching to the DECs was doomed, as no incentives or penalties were built into the system. Within a short time, other institutions realized that they could, with impunity, continue to offer off-campus courses. As a result there has been a rapid expansion in the number of universities doing so and in the number of courses being offered (Maticka, 1993). Many of these institutions have been ill-prepared to provide support for their off-campus students, particularly library support, and have had to pour considerable resources into establishing new services to meet the needs of these students.

Library services for off-campus students were given a considerable boost by the publication of an influential study in 1983 by Winter and Cameron, which had been commissioned by the federal government. The study surveyed a large number of students and for the first time in Australia set down a model for library provision. The major recommendations of the study were:

1. a reciprocal borrowing arrangement should be developed to allow off-campus students of any institution to borrow from the libraries of any university in Australia;
2. a national network of integrated study centers for off-campus students should be developed from which a range of services, including information services, could be provided to off-campus students of any university;
3. telephone access, free return postage of book loans and literature searches should be provided for off-campus students by the library of the university with which students are enrolled;
4. all staff, particularly those working in the evenings and weekends when off-campus students are most likely to visit their libraries, should be well-trained and knowledgeable about the library's off-campus services;
5. library staff should be involved in course development from the earliest stages to ensure references in course material are accurate and annotated, correct information about information services is included, and library material has been purchased to support the course.

At about the same time, the Distance Education Special Interest Group of the Library Association of Australia (DESIG) (1982) issued a set of guidelines for the minimum level of library service for off-campus students. The guidelines begin with the firm statement that "It is the responsibility of all institutions offering external studies to provide at least a base level of library service to their students commensurate with the library-related needs of their courses" (p. 7). The publication was structured as sets of recommendations together with questions which libraries might ask about their own level of service. Libraries wishing to apply the guidelines were able to work through these questions, assessing the degree to which they met the guidelines or actions which they needed to take in order to do so. The guidelines were used widely in the 1980s by libraries with off-campus students and at least one such library was able to obtain additional funding by demonstrating short-falls in their services (Crocker, 1986, p. 8)

DESIG has also held regular workshops and conferences and has acted as a pressure group independent of universities and colleges; for example, by publishing a manual listing the services provided by the various off-campus teaching institutions and distributing this manual to public libraries across the country (Crocker and Grimison, 1989).

C. Open Learning Australia

In the face of the failure of the DEC system, the Australian government tried a different approach to improving the efficiency and cost-effectiveness of off-campus teaching by establishing an open university. After a tendering process, 3-year funding was granted to an incorporated company, the Open Learning Agency of Australia Pty. Ltd. to provide open learning courses at undergraduate and postgraduate level at a reasonable cost within Australia and overseas (Open Learning Agency of Australia, 1996). The Agency, which trades as Open Learning Australia (OLA) acts essentially as a broker of courses which are taught by universities and technical colleges from across Australia; currently more than half of all Australian universities offer courses through OLA (Atkinson, 1996).

OLA offers courses in each of four study periods, beginning March, June, September, and December each year. Students enroll with OLA, but thereafter are in the hands of the teaching institution, which distributes course material, marks assignments, and conducts examinations. Students receive certificates of achievement from OLA which can be used to obtain credit in programs offered by other universities. OLA does not award degrees, although most participating universities accept OLA units towards their own degrees.

One of the features of OLA is the use of radio and television broadcasting to disseminate teaching material. Programs are broadcast on the publicly funded Australian Broadcasting Commission (ABC) networks which cover the country. Programs are produced by educational providers, some in collaboration with the broadcaster, or are documentary series produced for general viewing (for example, "The Long Search" series used in Religion Studies courses) or educational series purchased from elsewhere ("French in Action" used for French Language courses). In 1996 24 hours of Open Learning television programs were broadcast each week of the year (Perlgut, 1996).

OLA does not provide a library service directly. In fact, in the early stages of developing OLA's programs, it was assumed that a library service was unnecessary as it was expected that course providers would issue students with all the materials they would require. Lobbying by the library profession resulted in the government granting three million (Australian) dollars to OLA for library support as well as reserving a portion of unit registration fees for this purpose. Initially the library of the Gippsland campus of Monash University was awarded the contract to coordinate this support which was provided by the libraries of the course providers, some of which already had an off-campus student's library service. These libraries were paid a collection development fee for each student enrolled in a course being taught by their institution and a transaction fee for services provided, using a voucher system.

Following a review in 1994 by Nicholson *et al.*, the voucher system was abandoned, a librarian was appointed to the OLA staff for a 1-year period and participating libraries were paid a fee for each student registering as a user, together with a collection development fee on the same basis as before, although at a much-reduced level. OLA also provided funding for development projects, including a CD-ROM program on library skills which was produced by the University of Southern Queensland for sale to students. The program is aimed to teach generalized library use skills, recognizing that OLA students are using a range of libraries with different online public access catalogs, classification systems, and collections.

The system changes again in 1997. OLA's funding from the Australian government has come to an end, necessitating a review of resource allocation. Following a tender process in mid-1996, the University of South Australia was awarded the contract to provide an off-campus library service to all OLA students from March, 1997. This move should overcome some of the problems which OLA students have encountered in obtaining library services. Their use of library services is low compared to that of mainstream off-campus students (Nicholson, *et al.*, 1994), for a number of reasons. While each OLA study period is comparable in length to the semesters generally adopted by Australian universities, the lack of any break between the end of one study period and the beginning of the next imposes a very tight schedule for the supply of teaching material, effectively eliminating the lead-time which mainstream off-campus students usually enjoy, a period which allows students time to consider and plan their strategies in relation to matters such as library use. For the OLA student, the realization that additional resources are needed often comes so late in the study period that there is little or no time to arrange access to a suitable library. The large number of providers offering a library service placed students in the position of making a choice at short notice on the basis of fairly scanty information. To compound the problem, establishing borrowing rights at the chosen library was a bureaucratic process, requiring providing evidence of current enrollment in an OLA unit, filling out a form, and paying a fee. All of these factors conspired to discourage students from attempting to use the provider libraries, turning instead to public libraries or simply relying on the course material provided.

D. Engineering Education Australia

Engineering Education Australia (EEA) is a wholly owned subsidiary of the Institution of Engineers, Australia. It provides continuing education (award programs) and training (nonaward programs) to meet the needs of engineers wherever they live and work. Over 300 courses provided from Australian universities, technical colleges, and industry are available, including formal distance education courses, guided learning packages and workshops. Formal distance education courses lead to awards at the bachelor, diploma, and masters levels granted by Deakin University (a multicampus university with its headquarters in Geelong, a Victorian regional city), to EEA's own Graduate Diploma of Engineering or to a Technical and Further Education (TAFE) Diploma of Engineering. EEA courses may also be credited toward the Institution's continuing professional development requirements, with one course normally meeting an individual's requirements for a 3-year period. Although many of the courses available are taught by Deakin University, 12 other universities are also involved.

As with OLA, EEA students enroll through EEA but are thereafter taught and examined by the provider university and are presumably entitled to a library service from that university, if it provides one to off-campus students; several of the participating universities do not have significant mainstream off-campus programs. The service provided by Deakin University is the only one mentioned in EEA's literature (Engineering Education Australia, 1996).

E. Does Australia Have Virtual Universities?

In the establishment of virtual universities Australia has lagged behind the United States, despite its tradition of off-campus education at all levels. There are a number of factors contributing to this situation. Australian universities receive the majority of their funding from the federal government, so that there has been little opportunity or incentive to develop nontraditional universities outside the public system. During the 1980s there was considerable interest in and enthusiasm for the establishment of private universities in Australia, but in the event only two eventuated: Bond University in Queensland and Notre Dame in Western Australia, and both still struggle to attract sufficient students to be viable. Both are organized as traditional on-campus teaching universities. Within mainstream universities the demand for on-campus places had been intense until the early 1990s, providing little incentive for these institutions to look to nontraditional students to fill classes.

The development of Engineering Education Australia and other similar industry-based programs can be attributed to a change in government policy which required all employers with more than a minimal number of employees to allocate specific funding to staff development and training; whether these programs will continue without the training requirements of this policy is not clear.

The establishment of Open Learning Australia signaled a change in government policy in relation to tertiary education provision. While OLA does not grant its own awards, it has demonstrated that the model of an educational broker works in the Australian context and can attract students, at least at the level of fees which have been charged during its establishment phase. Teaching OLA courses has proved to many institutions which had not previously been involved in distance education that this is a viable form of educational delivery. Very recently many universities have developed or are interested in developing "virtual campuses" which range from World Wide Web homepages to credit courses delivered to students on-line, demonstrating a growing expertise in electronic teaching. At the same time, Australian libraries have made great advances in providing electronic resources for both on- and off-campus students.

In late 1996 Melbourne University announced its intended participation in a virtual university to be called Universitas 21, which will include universities in Britain, New Zealand, Australia, Canada, and the United States (Maslin, 1996). There is no doubt that other universities will follow this lead. While Australia does not yet have a full-fledged virtual university, it is likely that such a development is imminent.

IV. Virtual Universities in North America

In 1996 I was fortunate in receiving a study grant to travel to North America to investigate the role of libraries in virtual universities. The staffs of 10 institutions in California, Colorado, and British Columbia generously hosted my visits and gave their time, expertise, and insights. These 10 included mainstream universities, universities using cable and satellite television and electronic means for course delivery, and a virtual university in the making. Which of these are virtual universities?

A. A Virtual Development within a Mainstream University: University of California Extension

The University of California at Berkeley is a campus of a large, highly regarded, research-oriented university which focuses on on-campus teaching.

Perhaps not so well known are the activities of UC Extension which has been running continuing education courses for more than 100 years, initially as face-to-face courses around the San Francisco Bay area and more recently as interactive videoconferencing to sites in Berkeley, San Francisco, San Ramon, and Menlo Park since 1992. A half-million-dollar grant from the Alfred P. Sloan Foundation in 1993 and a further substantial grant in 1996 have enabled the development of online teaching, initially of the Certificate Program in Hazardous Materials Management. At present 25 courses are offered online with a further 150 planned by 1999.

UC Extension's Center for Media and Independent Learning (CMIL) is using the commercial Internet provider America Online as the delivery vehicle for delivering its online courses. Students receive printed course materials and may purchase textbooks through CMIL. Online services include "real time" discussions, e-mail, bulletin boards for group activities, and electronic submission of assignments. Using America Online relieves CMIL of the considerable responsibility of assisting students in arranging online access and providing continuing computer support.

No library service is provided to UC Extension students, although there is close liaison between the CMIL staff and the Library's Media Resources Center, as CMIL has an extensive video rental and sales business. It is expected that students will find information resources within their communities. As well, America Online provides some information resources and links to others on the Internet which could be useful for students. This low level of library support is typical of extension and continuing education programs in both Australia and the United States. While these programs are frequently kept at arms' length by their parent institutions, this need not be the case; at the University of New England, its commercial arm, UNE-Partnerships, has entered into a contract with the University Library under which their students receive the same library services as do mainstream off-campus students at no additional cost to these students.

B. Two Television Universities: The National Technological University and the Mind Extension University

The National Technological University (NTU) was founded in 1984 to serve the advanced educational needs of engineers, scientists, and technical managers and is a consortium of educational institutions and industry organisations. Its establishment was funded by a grant from the Sloan Foundation and from industry. NTU offers a range of instructional television courses taught by faculty in 47 engineering schools across the United States. Lectures are broadcast via satellite either live or from tapes to 975 earth stations throughout the United States and in 12 Pacific Rim countries. NTU had 1292 students enrolled in degree programs in May, 1996 and has conferred close to 1000 degrees since 1984. Around 100,000 students enroll in short courses each year.

In order to participate in NTU, universities must have had a video outreach program for at least 2 years and have the facilities to upload broadcasts. As masters-level courses in the United States do not need to be accredited, participating schools must have undergraduate courses accredited with ABET (the US engineering education accrediting body). An independent body (currently Purdue University) evaluates each course, and outstanding instructor awards are made annually. Instructors who perform badly and courses which have evaluated poorly are removed from the program.

Courses are delivered to television receive-only terminals in corporate sites. Sponsoring organizations provide classrooms, computer access, selected equipment, laboratories, telecommunications equipment, and educational personnel. Electronic mail and other more conventional communication media are the principal means of interaction between students and instructors (National Technological University, 1995).

NTU students are, for all intents and purposes, students of the institution teaching the course in which they are currently enrolled, even though NTU actually enrolls them and confers their degree. Given the very large number of courses, individual students may be dealing with a number of institutions during their period of enrollment with NTU. This has the potential to cause difficulties for library support, as many participating institutions do not provide an off-campus library service. NTU will provide letters of introduction to libraries upon request and it is expected that in most cases the student's employer will have a technical library which the student can use. While many participating organizations have very fine special libraries, this approach does throw responsibility for information provision, which is rightly NTU's, onto other organizations. Should NTU move beyond delivery to workplaces (and it has been experimenting with using community open access sites for the benefit of students whose employers do not participate in NTU), alternative information services will be required.

The Mind Extension University (ME/U) located in Denver, Colorado, is a nonprofit body within Jones International, Ltd., a corporate parent to 17 subsidiaries within the telecommunications industry, primarily related to television programming and cable television. ME/U delivers accredited programs at master, bachelor, associate and certificate levels to 26 million households in the United States. ME/U is essentially a clearinghouse for educational courses for which programs can be broadcast, selecting courses from the offerings of 12 accredited universities and colleges, publicizing them through the cable TV network and arranging initial enrollment. The participating institutions teach, examine, and grant awards. ME/U offers some student support (mainly electronic discussion groups), supplies teaching material, sells textbooks, and offers financial advice. Courses offered are chosen on the basis that they are complete awards, have a learner-centred approach, use multiple media, and are in subject areas of high demand (particularly business, culture and languages, health, and computing).

While most programs are broadcast on ME/U Knowledge TV, students may also elect to receive a videotape of each program; however, ME/U is consciously moving away from its video approach to a more multimedia one. There is growing use of voicemail; for example, the Regis University courses use it extensively. About half of all courses require students to have access to a computer. The Colorado Electronic Community College teaches an entirely online Associate of Arts degree through ME/U.

ME/U enrolls 5000–6000 students annually, including some international students. A targeted MBS program is being run for a group in Germany, and there are some programs broadcast in China and the UK.

Also within the Jones organization is the International University College. IUC was established in 1995 by Glenn Jones (the Jones International founder and president) who had become impatient with the slow progress being made in persuading participating universities to accept his model of learning. Through ME/U, IUC offers Arts in Business Communication at the Masters and Bachelors' levels. While still very much video based, the courses also have an online component. IUC has state approval to enroll students and to award degrees and is in the process of gaining accreditation.

Neither ME/U nor IUC provide a library service. ME/U expects participating universities and colleges to provide library services to the students enrolled in their programs, while the IUC publicity states: "Library resources are available for courses. Bibliographies supplied with the course materials identify appropriate publications, some or all of which may be available at your community college. In addition, International University College provides information on accessing reference resources through the Internet. The Dean's Office maintains a library liaison who assists students in obtaining library materials" (International University College, 1995, p. 13). In fact, in July, 1996, IUC did not employ a librarian nor had it any facilities for supplying library material to students, although it does have an arrangement with the University of Denver under which library services are provided to IUC students.

Since ME/U students typically enroll in full programs and therefore can be expected to be studying for lengthy periods with one institution (under the ME/U banner), there is the opportunity for the development of a relationship with the library of that institution. ME/U's responsibility, then, is to ensure that participating institutions do make adequate provision for such services to ME/U students.

C. An Electronic University: The University of Phoenix Online Campus

The University of Phoenix (UP) has 47 campuses, of which 45 are on-campus teaching institutions located mainly throughout the southwestern United States. A conventional distance education campus operates from Phoenix, while the Online Campus is located in San Francisco. UP was founded as a private university in 1976 aimed specifically at adult students and at around 36,000 students is now the second largest private university in the United States. The founder, Dr. Sperling, is still the chair of the Apollo Group, which also includes IPD (offering continuing education courses through existing universities in the eastern United States) and the Western International University, which was purchased recently.

The University of Phoenix Online Campus (UPO) has around 1500 students, including 50–60 overseas students. An international office has been established and a global MBA program was to be launched in January, 1997. Currently, UPO offers bachelor's and master's programs in business and management.

The University controls the development and teaching of courses very tightly through centralized course design and mentoring of new instructors. All teaching is experiential and group based, with around 12 students in each online group and no more than 20 in an on-campus group. Online courses begin whenever a viable sized group has enrolled, usually monthly. Each group meets weekly and works cooperatively; this includes students of the Online Campus. Each class runs for 5, 6, or 10 weeks and has stringent requirements for regular participation by both students and faculty. Students log in using either a modem or the Internet. Upon login, the software downloads all new material for that student and uploads anything the student has prepared for submission, so that online time is short. As well as class material, students have access to discussion groups, e-mail to the faculty or other students, and bulletin boards. Assignments are transmitted electronically.

UP does not have a library at any of its campuses, although some have appointed librarians to their staff. The Learning Resource Center (LRC) has a staff of nine located in Phoenix and provides a virtual library of Internet based links to information resources including a number of electronic databases. The various campuses have public terminals which students may use to consult the LRC and UPO students can access it directly. The LRC will undertake subject searches and will deliver photocopies of journal articles by fax or mail. Links are also provided to some commercial document delivery services (e.g., CARL UnCover) from which students may obtain journal articles directly (at their own expense). The accrediting agency (North-Central Association) had some difficulty with this approach to a library service, but has accepted that it meets students' needs.

The UPO model is a good one for a virtual university of this type, except that it is unable to provide book loans, effectively cutting off access to a very large part of recorded information. However, the employment of professional library staff opens up the opportunity for their input to course development and design and for the provision of policy advice in relation to information provision. Since all UPO students must have computers and modems, the electronic services provided by the LRC are appropriate and can be accessed by students everywhere, including overseas.

D. A Virtual University in the Making: The Western Governors University

In June, 1996 the Governors of the western states of the United States signed an agreement to establish a virtual university to be called the Western Governors University (WGU). The Western Interstate Commission for Higher Education (WICHE), based in Boulder, Colorado, is a regional organization representing 15 western states and aims to promote and facilitate resource sharing. Through its subordinate body, the Western Cooperative for Educational Telecommunications (WCET), WICHE is heavily involved in the planning and development of the Western Governors University.

WGU is very much a political development. Population growth in the western states is outstripping higher education places at a time when most state governments are unable or unwilling to expand places in universities and particularly to add new programs. At the same time, many people live in very isolated areas and are unable to participate in on-campus study. The growth of the high-technology industry in the Pacific states particularly has lead to an increased demand for industry-focused training and for the recognition of prior learning through on-the-job training. All of these factors have had an impact on the political process, leading to a cooperative and innovative response.

A major feature of WGU will be its online catalog which will relate course content to skills assessment and will store a profile of each student to allow matching of course content, examination locations, and other useful information. The pilot catalog is being developed by IBM in conjunction with WCET. WGU intends to begin enrolling students in the summer of 1997, acting as a broker initially, although it may award its own degrees later.

Planning for support services has begun and will be assisted by a federal grant which WCET has received to draft standards for student support for electronic teaching. This is to be a 3-year study and will include consideration of library services. A consultant was appointed in late 1996 to advise on planning library support services.

Whether the WGU will become a reality remains to be seen. Issues such as credit transfer, tuition fees, maintenance of the catalog, support services, and administration in general need to be resolved. At a more fundamental level the philosophy underpinning WGU has been challenged by the view that the completion of a miscellany of courses from different providers, including industry, does not constitute a university education. It has also been argued that such an approach does not produce graduates with the work skills that will be required in the future (Ashworth, 1996). Already, the largest state in WICHE, California, has decided not to participate, choosing instead to develop its own virtual university (Blumenstyk, 1996). Nevertheless, the WGU is a bold attempt to address some of the pressing issues in higher education in the region.

E. A Canadian Virtual University: The Open Learning Agency

The Open Learning Agency, located in Burnaby, British Columbia is a non-profit fully accredited educational institution which provides learning and training opportunities to British Columbians anywhere. The Open University (a division within the Open Learning Agency) offers programs of study leading to university and associate degrees. Other divisions offer programs at K–12, college, and workplace skills levels. The Open Learning Agency provides around 250 courses itself and brokers another 250 courses offered by Simon Fraser University, University of British Columbia, and Victoria University. Television broadcasts, videoconferencing, electronic media including CDROM and the Internet, video and audio cassettes, and traditional print materials are used to deliver course materials.

The Open Learning Agency manages the Electronic Library Network (ELN), which provides access to the collections of 64 postsecondary and public libraries throughout British Columbia. ELN also allows access to a range of electronic databases and online document requesting and rapid delivery services. ELN therefore allows resource sharing in a way which particularly advantages off-campus students. All students who have an Open Learning Agency computer account have direct access to ELN.

Open Learning Agency students receive a service based on the Simon Fraser University Library, but provided by Open Learning Agency staff based there. The Open Learning Agency covers the staffing costs involved and pays a fee to Simon Fraser University for the right to use the collection on behalf of its students. The Agency has its own library which services the professional needs of its staff. The librarian has a high profile within the institution with responsibility for a number of areas beyond the library; for example, copyright. Several former library staff have moved to other positions within the organization such as instructional design, which has incidentally strengthened the library's standing in the organization. Management of the ELN ensures the

Open Learning Agency plays a major role in the development and management of information provision to tertiary students throughout the province.

The interrelationship between University of British Columbia, Simon Fraser University, Victoria University, and the Open Learning Agency in the provision of educational opportunities for off-campus students and the high degree of cooperation in information provision ensures greater access to scarce resources for the community. The model of providing a service through a contract with another library is an excellent one for virtual universities to consider, especially those brokering courses from other institutions. Students are not required to make choices between libraries, the virtual university is spared the expense of developing a collection and associated services, while the host library is recompensed for the use of its facilities. Dedicated staff ensures that the virtual university students receive a high priority and are not swamped by competition from the host university's own students.

V. Virtual Universities and Their Libraries

Distance education has been a part of tertiary education long enough for both good library practice and a considerable body of literature to have developed; the second edition of the standard bibliography on the area contains more than 5000 entries (Slade and Kascus, 1996). This literature, however, addresses the issue of library support for conventional distance education. The universities described above present new models for teaching at a distance at the tertiary level, raising new problems for library support. In each case, the provision which has (or has not) been made for information services is highlighted. Of concern to librarians will be the low level of such provision, a level which is typical in many similar institutions in North America and Australia.

A. Information Literacy

Why should this be of concern, when educators clearly believe that such provision is not essential? The world is rapidly moving into what has been termed the "information age" (George and Luke, 1995), in which lifelong learning will be the norm, as people find they need to retrain for new careers or to develop additional skills for their current careers in order to remain in or to join the workforce. Information literacy is a skill, the development of which is an essential part of university education. An institution which is concerned about the fostering of its students' information skills will aim to produce graduates who are able to recognize their need for information, be able to find suitable information in a variety of community resources (electronic, print, and human), and make an informed use of this information (Doyle, 1994).

The acquisition of these skills is much easier for on-campus students than it is for their off-campus peers. The opportunity to visit their institution's library frequently, to seek assistance from library staff, to review a range of information sources and to receive informal guidance from peers and teachers are all denied off-campus students or are at best available in a very restricted way (George and Love, 1995). Librarians in mainstream universities accept a central role in developing information literacy skills of their students: similar provision must be made for students of virtual universities. For institutions which require off-campus students to visit the campus regularly, as is the case at the University of New England, opportunities exist to deliver face-to-face information literacy training. This situation, however, is very rare and will become nonexistent in virtual universities, by definition. Alternative strategies include the development of electronic and print training packages (such as that produced for Open Learning Australia), inclusion of material in course packages, and, most importantly, training course developers and teachers in the teaching of these skills.

B. The Role of the Internet as an Information Source for Virtual University Students

It is often argued that virtual universities do not require libraries. The argument usually centers on the notion that resources freely available through the Internet will meet students' needs.

There are a number of problems with this approach. The Internet is a huge and unstructured mass of information. To search the Internet successfully requires skill and practice (and considerable time online, for which most students will be required to pay). Many electronic resources which students will find on the Internet are available only at a cost. The considerable range of bibliographic databases, which parallel the printed bibliographies which formed the backbone of literature searches in the past, are extremely expensive and can only be accessed by authorized users. Unless virtual universities subscribe to these services or make some other arrangements, they will not be available to their students.

Even when students are able to access electronic bibliographic databases, there still remains the issue of obtaining the text of the items identified. Students will have to resort to commercial document supply services, at a higher cost than obtaining the same items from a library. While much material is now available in full text, most is not refereed in the same way as are articles which appear in scholarly printed journals. This situation will change as electronic journals become more accepted, but at present there is a problem for students in assessing the quality of material retrieved.

C. Library Services Provided by Virtual Universities Today

The institutions described above share a common lack of the provision of a traditional university-style library service. Some (for instance, The University of Phoenix Online Campus and Open Learning Australia) have adopted solutions which acknowledge the needs that students have for material beyond those supplied directly to them in their course packages and the obligation which any university has to arrange library support for its students. The traditional role of the university library, however, goes beyond the provision of specific books, journal articles, and other materials to students enrolled in courses currently being taught. University libraries collect materials in subject areas in which their institutions might be expected to teach in the future and in areas in which the institution does not teach, but which provide basic information as background to areas in which teaching does occur. They also collect materials to support the development and redevelopment of new and existing courses. An important role is seen for the collection of materials to support research by academic staff and higher degree students and the provision of access to these materials nationally and internationally as a contribution to scholarship worldwide. Finally, library collections are developed systematically, by reference to collection development policies, through selection by library staff on the basis of reviews and citations in reputable journals and monographs, and by academic staff drawing upon their extensive knowledge of their field of expertise. A library collection is an entity which has coherence and relevance to the community which it serves and is built to meet the needs of its clients, in stark contrast to the all-inclusive, unstructured mass of resources provided by the Internet.

Virtual universities will not develop large physical library collections and in fact the evidence to date suggests that they may be reluctant to even meet their basic obligation to provide for the immediate needs of currently enrolled students. While the wide range of electronic databases is now available allows virtual universities to provide bibliographic information reasonably easily, by necessity they must rely heavily, at least for the next few years, on conventional libraries for the supply of books and journals. While the range of full-text electronic material will increase rapidly in the near future, issues of access to proprietary material will remain unresolved and in any case the vast majority of material already in print is unlikely to be converted to electronic form in even the long term. The lack of an extensive research collection will deprive academic staff (if the virtual university employs any) of an essential resource which they require for the development of courses and for their own research activities.

Virtual universities must consider carefully their students' information needs and make arrangements for these needs to be met in a way which students will find easy and economical to use. The precise way will depend on the structure of the organization, but it is important that students have barrier-free access to an information service which has accepted responsibility for meeting their needs. The situation where students are forced to deal with a number of different libraries must be avoided. At the National Technological University, for example, students could be placed in the situation of having to form a relationship with a different library for each course in which they enroll. This approach is certain to discourage use and to compound the difficulties which all students using a library at a distance face. An approach to such a situation would be for NTU to devise a "front end" which would act as an intermediary, obtaining material on behalf of students from the participating libraries in the way that the University of Phoenix Learning Resource Center obtains material from a number of sources on behalf of students.

For most institutions, a relationship with one library with a well-established off-campus service will be the most economical and satisfactory arrangement. This relationship must be well funded so that the supplying library has a strong incentive to perform well. The Open Learning Agency model of paying for staff to carry out the service and, in addition, contributing collection development funds seems to be an excellent approach.

D. The Role of Librarians in Virtual Universities Today

The lack of a library may deprive the students and staff of the virtual university, not only of the physical collection, but also of the professional expertise of library staff. The Vice-Chancellor of Melbourne University, Professor Alan Gilbert (1995), said of universities: "Such complex and holistic institutions operate best as genuine communities in which personal interactions, informal as well as formal, shape the learning environment." While he was writing primarily of the interaction between academic staff and students, librarians also contribute to this shaping, at many levels and in many ways.

As information specialists, librarians are in the best position to advise instructional designers and teachers on issues such as access to information, the quality of information sources and patterns of student behaviour in seeking and using information. Librarians are also skilled in teaching information seeking skills, both directly through training courses and packages and through information incorporated into course material.

As advocates for students and as representatives of their institutions, librarians are best able to negotiate with the libraries of other institutions for access to resources and as partners in joint projects such as the Electronic Library Network in British Columbia.

Even if a virtual university chooses not to develop its own library service, the contribution that librarians are able to make in many ways is invaluable; it is in the best interests of virtual universities to employ library staff directly or to at least obtain this expertise through periodic consultancies.

E. Challenges for Librarians

All of the preceding argument in support of the central role of libraries in virtual universities presupposes that libraries are able to provide an appropriate service to their students. The experience of the University of Oregon's participation in a project to add Internet resources to the library's collection (by including URLs in their catalog) is not unusual. Despite careful policy and procedural development, the project added few resources to the online catalog mainly because of ambivalence among subject specialists regarding the desirability of using the catalog as a gateway to Internet resources (Watson, 1996). Such a response is not unusual, as librarians fight to retain adequate funding for existing services in times of shrinking resources for tertiary education. Equally, administrators of virtual universities working on tight budgets are reluctant to commit resources to the development of information services themselves or to contracts with other providers.

It is particularly important that librarians take a proactive stance on the issues of information provision and information literacy for students of virtual universities. Pressure from librarians was effective in forcing the Australian Government and Open Learning Australia to provide a library service for OLA students; similar pressure is being brought to bear on the Western Governors University. We must make clear to administrators and academic staff of virtual universities the need for access to information and the role which librarians can play in providing this information. We should be setting up excellent electronic services that will provide structured access to relevant information for our students.

Librarians should also be looking to the provision of suitable resources on the Internet. We particularly need to lobby commercial publishers to ensure that good access to scholarly material is possible at a price which universities and individuals can afford.

Librarians must be vigilant in countering the argument that universities of the future will not need libraries. While it is true that many students, both on and off- campus, pass through our universities without ever making use of library services or resources (Mays, 1985), we are failing our institutions and our students if we succumb to the view that a book of readings and a Web browser are all an undergraduate needs.

There is no doubt that virtual universities will continue to develop. They challenge the traditional model of university organization and teaching and will no doubt influence that model profoundly. The challenge for librarians is to ensure that we continue to play a central role in university life, as professionals with expertise which is essential if excellent teaching and research are to occur, as advocates on behalf of our students and academic staff in information matters and as custodians and disseminators of knowledge.

Acknowledgments

I am greatly indebted to the Australian Library and Information Association and to Open Learning Australia for their financial support, without which this study would have been impossible. Descriptions of individual institutions included in this paper are based largely on personal communications from officers of those institutions, who gave generously of their time and knowledge. The conclusions drawn in this paper, however, are entirely those of the author.

References

Ashworth, K. W. (1996). Virtual universities can produce only virtual learning. *Chronicle of Higher Education*, September 6, p. A88.

Ashton, J. (1971). *Out of the Silence.* Investigator Press, Adelaide.

Atkinson, E. (1996). Open/flexible learning and the Open Learning Institute. In *Open Learning '96*, pp. 45–48. Open Learning Network, Brisbane, Queensland.

Blainey, G. (1966). *The Tyranny of Distance.* Sun Books, Melbourne.

Blumenstyk, G. (1996). Shunning west's 'virtual university,' Ca. will offer own courses on line. *Chronicle of Higher Education*, October 11, p. A34.

Crocker, C. (1986). Guidelines and guidance: Galvanising the library service. In *Library Services in Distance Education.* South Australian College of Advanced Education, Adelaide.

Crocker, C., and Grimison, C. (1989). *Library Services for External Students: A Guide.* Library Association of Australia Special Interest Group on Distance Education, Armidale, NSW.

Dawkins, J. (1988). *Higher Education: Policy Statement.* Australian Government Publishing Service, Canberra.

Doyle, C. S. (1994). *Information Literacy in an Information Society.* ERIC Clearinghouse on Information and Technology, Syracuse, NY.

Engineering Education Australia (1996). *July-December 1996 Prospectus.* Engineering Education Australia, North Melbourne.

George, R., and Love, A. (1995). The culture of the library in open and distance education contexts. *Australian Academic and Research Libraries* **26,** 129–136.

George, R., and Luke, R. (1995). The critical place of information literacy in the trend towards flexible delivery in higher education contexts. Paper delivered at the Learning for Life Conference, Adelaide. Available: http://www.lgu.ac.uk/deliberations/flex.learning/rigmor_paper.html

Gilbert, A. (1995). The virtual university. *University Gazette*, Autumn, p. 5.

Hutchison, C. (1996). Snares in the charmed circle. *Times Higher Education Supplement* **1223,** iv-v.

International University College (1995). *Graduate Bulletin.* IUC, Englewood, CO.

Library Association of Australia. Distance Education Special Interest Group (1982). *Guidelines for Library Services to External Students.* LAA, Ultimo, NSW.

Lim, E. H. T. (1992). Multicampus library operations: The Victorian experience. In *Australian Tertiary Libraries: Issues for the 1990s* (C. Steele, ed.). Auslib Press, Adelaide.

Maslin, G. (1996). The future is virtual, says Melbourne VC. *Campus Review*, **6**, (November 27), 6.

Maticka, M. (1992). Distance education and libraries. In *Australian Tertiary Libraries: Issues for the 1990s* (C. Steele, ed.). Auslib Press, Adelaide.

Maticka, M. (1993). The effects of the establishment of distance education centres on the duplication and diversity of external higher education courses. Thesis, Master of Distance Education, University of South Australia, Adelaide.

Mays, A. H. (1985). The centrality of library services in informational support patterns of undergraduate students: a study of users and non-users at Deakin University Library. Thesis, Master of Librarianship, Monash University, Melbourne.

Nader, J. C. (1995). *Prentice Hall's Illustrated Dictionary of Computing*, 2nd ed. Prentice Hall, Sydney.

National Technological University (1995). *Annual Report 1994–95*. NTU, Fort Collins, CO.

Nicholson, F., McIntyre, B., and Findlay, M. (1994). *Open Learning Australia Library Review*. OLA, Melbourne.

Open Learning Agency of Australia (1996). *Open Learning Annual Report 1995*. Open Learning Agency of Australia, Melbourne.

Perlgut, D. (1996) The future of educational television on ABC TV. In *Open Learning '96*, pp. 438-442 Open Learning Network, Brisbane, Queensland.

Slade, A. L., and Kascus, M. A. (1996). *Library Services for Off-Campus and Distance Education: Second Annotated Bibliography*. Canadian Library Association, Vancouver.

Small, I. W. (1978). External studies in Australia: Past and present. Dissertation, Master of Educational Administration, University of New England, Armidale.

Tiffin, J., and Rajasingham, L. (1995). *In Search of the Virtual Class*. Routledge, London.

Watson, M. (1996). *The Ambivalent Library*, Field Report, OCLC Internet Cataloguing Project Colloquium, Dublin, Ohio. Available: http://www.oclc.org/oclc/man/colloq/watson/fieldrep.htm.

Winter, A., and Cameron, M. (1983). *External Students and their Libraries*. Deakin University, Geelong, Victoria.

Taming the Internet

Metadata, A Work in Progress

Holley R. Lange
Colorado State University Libraries
Fort Collins, Colorado 80523

B. Jean Winkler
Colorado State University Libraries
Fort Collins, Colorado 80523

I. Introduction

She types in "METADATA," and the computer grinds away, finally responding: "You found 6010 relevant documents from a total of 60,434,860 indexed Web pages."[1] She takes a deep breath and begins to browse through the list, overwhelmed by the numbers. Over and over during the course of a day, in the United States and around the world, searchers have similar experiences. Each day the number of searchable files available via the Internet increases, exploding at nearly unimaginable rates. What is the solution to taming this rapidly expanding mass of information, providing searchers a reasonable expectation for efficiently discovering and retrieving the information they seek?

It is quickly obvious that traditional cataloging cannot be the answer to locating all the information on the Internet, today most popularly through the World Wide Web, even if librarians wanted to take that approach. How could anyone catalog 60 million items, many of which change daily, and many of which do not merit traditional cataloging? As comparison, the Library of Congress contains 16 million books and 100 million other items collected over its 200 year life span, although many still lack full cataloging; the library grows at a rate of 7000 items per working day (Library of Congress, 1996a). OCLC's (Online Computer Library Center) online catalog, representing the combined efforts of thousands of libraries over a quarter century, contains fewer than 40,000,000 records.[2]

[1] Lycos (1/3/97).
[2] Over 36,000,000 as of 1/3/97.

0065-2830/97 $25.00

Despite the size of the Internet, librarians are cataloging some of its resources in traditional ways and incorporating those cataloging records in their online catalogs, but they are also working toward other solutions as well. Simultaneously, often in parallel, but sometimes cooperatively with librarians, computer experts are seeking technical solutions that may provide effective ways to search, discover, and retrieve files on the Internet. One proposed approach to capturing and perhaps taming this mass of "information," at least enough to provide effective discovery of available resources, is through the use of metadata. Metadata are sets of descriptors used or proposed for use to describe electronic resources. If generally implemented, these standardized data elements, perhaps presented as part of the electronic file itself, might then be the focus of various current and future search tools and perhaps the basis for more detailed and traditional cataloging records.

The following pages will summarize ongoing efforts to develop descriptive standards, or "metadata," for electronic resources. Based on a review of the literature, both print and electronic, we provide a background to "cataloging" the Internet, with particular emphasis on use of metadata in the electronic environment. While the focus is on library and library-related initiatives, we note efforts in other communities as well. We summarize efforts now underway to investigate the most appropriate approaches to metadata, comment on some of the actual and potential problems involved in metadata creation and standardization, and reflect on the role of the library and librarian in this future world of information description and retrieval.

II. A Definition

Beyond and before the current growth of the Internet via the World Wide Web, computer experts and others in a variety of disciplines worked to better describe and so better manage electronic resources in their own disciplines. Although librarians might consider these descriptions not unlike cataloging, the computer world has a vocabulary all its own. Perhaps that is why the term "metadata" has more appeal there than "cataloging." As Larsgaard notes: "It is ironic that information derived by cataloging had to be called something else—metadata—before noncatalogers dealt with it" (Larsgaard, 1996, p. 19).

The concept of metadata has been defined by many, but the essence of the definition is constant and straightforward. Most basically metadata are "data about data," or data elements used to describe or represent electronic resources. The primary function of metadata is to aid a user in locating desired and relevant data, "to identify data which may satisfy the requirements of the user, and to store information about its location, content, and quality relative to the interests and situation of the user" (Madsen, *et al.*, 1994, pp. 237–238). It can provide information about an entire resource or only parts of it, but it "promotes sharing, reuse, and interoperability of data including information to help locate, access, browse, clean, and aggregate databases" (Cammarata *et al.*, 1994, p. 30). The data may accompany or be separate from the resource, but it enhances search precision, retrieval, management, and control of the resource (Hakala, *et al.*, 1996). Metadata may take the form of an index or template, and may describe format, multimedia content, location, or note any access fees (Hudgins-Bonafield, 1995, p. 104). Technical information appearing as metadata may include the capture process, information on the current and other versions, and use restrictions and means to gain permission for use or reuse (Erway, 1996). Metadata may also contain information on data accuracy as needed to establish the "pedigree" of the resource (Lide, 1995, pp. 33–34). Metadata should be simple, but expansive, and should assist searchers in locating and assessing a resource. Metadata is almost a hybrid of title page and catalog card, but one that also includes the technical information necessary to describe and use an electronic resource.

III. The Beginnings

The traditional catalog card, capturing the essence of a book or journal in a few lines, could be considered metadata. But even this descriptive essence had its roots in antiquity. Among the earliest known "cataloged" libraries was that of Assurbanipal at Nineveh in the 7th century B.C. (Kramer, 1967, p. 123). His library of clay tablets was grouped into rooms by subject. Within those rooms the tablets were stored in earthen jars placed in rows on shelves. Each jar had an identification tag indicating its proper location on the shelf, and each room had a list of the works contained in it on the wall near the door. A more descriptive listing of works within a room was also kept by the door, which included: title, location, number of lines in the work, and number of tablets it filled, as well as significant subdivisions within the work (Harris, 1995, pp. 20–21). Current library cataloging records include much of the same information, gathered and standardized based on the Anglo American Cataloging Rules (AACR2) (Gorman and Winkler, 1988) and placed in a MARC[3] framework. The online catalog, based on the catalog card, but often manipulated through the versatility of the MARC format, presents this same information on the computer. Resources accessed through the World Wide Web are certainly more numerous by many millions than Assurbanipal's

[3] MAchine Readable Cataloging (MARC) is a set of standards for identifying, storing, and communicating cataloging information.

library and even than all but the largest existing libraries, but these resources lack a descriptive standard to assist document discovery or retrieval.

Although the container for information has changed from clay, to parchment, to paper, to digital file, an individual's basic approach to information seeking has remained constant—searchers want to know what an item is and what it is about. Adding one more constant, how to find the item, we have a basic triumvirate for locating and retrieving resources. Perhaps this awareness, that there is a constancy in our approach to information retrieval, will help as we confront the somewhat overwhelming mass of electronically available information.

The Internet, developed as ARPAnet by the Department of Defense after World War II and during the following Cold War period, has been in existence for a number of years, but its recent public and much expanded phase has been explosive (Diamond and Bates, 1995). Although the world of the Internet, particularly the World Wide Web, developed outside of any traditional library organizational or cataloging structure, it was not without notice of the library world, as libraries and librarians made early use of such electronic resources. The World Wide Web, "a global hypertext system that uses the Internet as its transport mechanism" (Pfaffenberger, 1995, p. 564), became increasingly popular with the introduction of graphical Web browsers such as Mosaic and NetScape in the early 1990s. They allowed easy access to and presentation of documents incorporating text, images, and sound, and the Web has seen phenomenal growth since 1993 (Weibel, 1995b, pp. 7–10).

Advances in computer science over the past 25 years underlay metadata developments in other ways. As storage and access of data moved from magnetic tapes, to disk storage with direct rather than linear access, a database management system was needed. As users had more direct access to and control of the data, more information on the data themselves was required. This wide storage of data and varied access led to a demand for summary data about these databases (Inmon, 1992, pp. 2–11). The term metadata began to appear in the literature by the early 1980s, first in relation to these database management systems. According to Inmon, "Metadata has been a part of the information processing milieu for as long as there have been programs and data" (Inmon, 1992, p. 88). And although the Library of Congress authority record for "metadata" bears a recent date, an informational note on it states that the term was coined in the early 1960s.[4]

The appearance of the Web and the availability of many unique resources there resulted in a changing role for the information user, for on the Internet an individual might create, present ("publish"), remove, search, or change files and there that same individual also encounters (or finds missing) files created,

[4] Library of Congress Authority Record Number: ARN 4035768.

presented, changed, or removed by a host of other individuals, individuals often operating without apparent rules, common purposes, or standards. These changes are profound, so much so that Young and Peters suggest that this emerging Internet "library" may more closely approach the concept of the Alexandrian Library: "In the electronic age perhaps something approaching self-sufficiency of collections, together with access, will be possible. And as the original Alexandrian Library was conceived to house and place under bibliographic control the graphic record of antiquity, we are now perhaps in the process of reinventing the Alexandrian Library to realize the potential of the third millennium" (Young and Peters, 1996, p. 38). The Internet library does afford an individual a sense of self-sufficiency, but how are these individuals finding information, and what responsibility do librarians or possibly the authors/creators of the resources have in organizing this new "library"?

While there is wide variety in the quality of materials available on the Internet, there is much of value, much unique, and often in many arenas this is where the early discussions, initial papers, and new ideas are proposed and developed. There is also wide agreement that access to the information on the Internet is unorganized, and there is consensus that searching on the Web is imprecise. Obviously, material that cannot be located might almost not exist. In fact, Floridi comments that "there is more knowledge on the Internet than we can access" (Floridi, 1996, p. 49). Although there are many advantages in searching on the Web, with its ease of use and the easy integration of information through hyperlinks, browsing is not an effective means for locating specific information (Neuss and Kent, 1995, p. 973).

With the rapid growth of the World Wide Web, there is an acknowledged need for a more refined method to sift through files, so they may be "discovered" or "retrieved." Some believe technological efforts underway will be sufficient to solve current problems in searching the Internet, and computer experts have it fully in focus. As a recent article in *PC World* notes: "On the Internet, fortunately where there's a need, there's an eager programmer—or, increasingly, an entrepreneur—waiting to fill it" (Scoville, 1996, p. 128). And, in fact, many current searching tools have resulted from such responses. Some of these search tools now in use organize sites into directories by topic that allow a searcher to browse by category (e.g., Yahoo[5]). Other search tools, or engines (e.g., Lycos, InfoSeek[6]), collect Universal Resource Locators (URLs) into databases that have been located through Web crawlers, or spiders. These gather more information than just the URL, creating an index that may be based on URLs, titles within a document, first lines of text, or frequently occurring words. Some search tools index all the words in any

[5] Yahoo, The Yahoo! Corporation. Available: http://www.yahoo.com.

[6] Lycos, Lycos Inc. Available: http://www.lycos.com; InfoSeek. Available: http://www.infoseek.com.

given document (e.g., Open Text Index) (Scoville, 1996, p. 127).[7] Other, somewhat newer tools, called meta or mega search engines, simultaneously send search requests to several individual search engines at one time (e.g., Savvy Search, MetaCrawler)(Notess, 1996, p. 36).[8] Overall, there is an inconsistency in approach which leads to an unpredictability of result—only the most enlightened searcher will fully understand the search mechanism of the particular tool they use, and many may well be perplexed by the results and their apparent differences. As Scoville notes, "While the size of the database determines the number of hits it delivers, the quality of the indexing is a major factor in determining how many of those hits are relevant to your search" (Scoville, 1996, p. 128). For example, the same search on the term "Metadata" that resulted in 6010 "hits" on Lycos resulted in 16,193 on InfoSeek, 2074 on Magellan, and 5 sites on Yahoo.[9]

While it may be impossible, as well as unwise, to catalog everything on the Internet, a cataloging approach in the form of metadata has been suggested as a way to help users identify the information they seek. With more complete descriptions of resources available, whether autogenerated, author generated, or otherwise constructed, appropriately designed search engines will have more complete information on which to build their results. A common structure for such metadata is needed to guard against a virtual Tower of Babel on the Internet, and there are numerous efforts in process to refine and standardize the data used to describe information resources. Statisticians, geographers, environmentalists, commercial vendors, archivists, digital media specialists, humanities scholars, librarians, and others all have metadata-like initiatives in various stages of development.

IV. Cataloging and Metadata

A. Traditional Cataloging in New Arenas

The appearance of computer files in their various forms led to involvement of library personnel, first in cataloging of machine-readable and microcomputer files, then in cataloging Internet files, and most recently in discussions about the development and use of metadata to describe digital resources.

As prologue to Internet cataloging, and beginning with a demand to catalog machine-readable data files, catalogers studied the nature of these files and then developed rules for describing them. These rules first appeared in the second edition of the Anglo-American Cataloging Rules (Gorman and

[7] Open Text Index. Available: http://www.opentext.com/.

[8] SavvySearch. Available: http://savvy.cs.colostate.edu:2000; MetaCrawler. Available: http://www.metacrawler.com.

[9] Searches carried out on 1/3/97.

Winkler, 1978). The following year the Library of Congress began work on a MARC format for machine-readable data files, which was approved in late 1981. Similar work was undertaken with the appearance of microcomputer files, with 1984 guidelines being issued to assist librarians in their cataloging, based on the existing AACR2 Chapter 9 (American Library Association, Resources and Technical Services Division, 1984; Dodd and Sandberg-Fox, 1985, pp. 1–5). It is not surprising, then, that with the appearance and growing popularity of electronic files on the Internet, that catalogers and cataloging agencies became involved in experimenting with, examining, and developing guidelines for cataloging them in an attempt to augment what is currently a rather serendipitous approach to resource retrieval on the Internet.

One of the first formalized or structured projects by librarians to catalog electronic information on the Internet was the Internet Resource Project sponsored by the OCLC Office of Research in 1991–1992. The project staff collected over 1500 examples of electronic files, text, data, and software. The experiment included a test collection of 300 electronic files which were used by a group of volunteer librarians to determine whether the existing US-MARC format and cataloging rules could accommodate the creation of records for the electronic resources found on the Internet. Thirty-eight librarians participated in the experiment and contributed an estimated 500 hours of cataloging during May and June of 1992 (Jul, 1992; Dillon, *et al.*, 1993). The results showed that even though some problems were encountered, in general the USMARC format and AACR2 cataloging rules could be used with some slight modifications. The most significant deficiency identified was the inability to link bibliographic records directly with the remote resources they described. This led to the creation of a new USMARC field, the 856 (Electronic Location and Access), that most frequently contains the URL for a resource, and with the appropriate system a searcher is able to "click" on the URL in the cataloging record and access the resource. This field continues to be refined (Dillon and Jul, 1996; Library of Congress, 1996c).

Following this preliminary effort, OCLC initiated a 2-year project in 1994, "Building a Catalog of Internet-Accessible Materials." The goal was to create such a catalog using USMARC format bibliographic records incorporating the 856 field, thus providing a description enhanced by location, including the potential for direct access to these remote resources. Again a call went out for libraries interested in volunteering staff time to identify, select, and catalog these items (OCLC, 1994). A total of 231 libraries contributed over 4000 bibliographic records by the close of the project. As of December, 1996, Intercat contained 8266 records and is growing at an accelerated rate (E. Jul, personal communication, December 1996). The project effort demonstrated not only that the USMARC format and AACR2 could be used to describe Internet files, but that there were many valuable resources to be cataloged on the Internet. Problems identified included the time-consuming aspects of this work and the inability as yet to automatically transfer data existing in a computer file into appropriate USMARC fields (Library of Congress, 1996d). A mid-project colloquium was held in February, 1996, with reports from participants, but it also included a number of position papers addressing broader interests on Internet resources and cataloging (OCLC, 1996). A final report on project findings is to be published in early 1997 (E. Jul, personal communication, December, 1996).

Two guides to cataloging electronic resources that were developed to aid catalogers working with these less familiar formats are Hoogcarspel's (1994) *Guidelines for Cataloging Monographic Electronic Texts at the Center for Electronic Texts in the Humanities* and Olson's (1995) *Cataloging Internet Resources: A Manual and Practical Guide.* The former was compiled to assist in cataloging the resources included in the Rutgers Inventory of Machine-Readable Texts in the Humanities and is focused on RLIN (Research Libraries Information Network of the Research Libraries Group). Olson's guide was widely used in OCLC's 1994 project noted above. Both works cover AACR2's Chapter 9, providing explanations and examples.

B. Metadata Development

Even though these projects demonstrated the functionality of the USMARC format and AACR2 for electronic resources particularly in providing access to specific resources important to individual libraries, they did not solve the problem of how librarians could possibly catalog the growing number of materials on the Internet, nor did they address the interests of other communities in recording specialized data that might be required in addition to the traditional cataloging description itself. Metadata became a focus in both library and nonlibrary universes as a possible solution to these problems. The general practice, still the case, was that each discipline, product, or purpose worked to define a specific, tailored set of data elements to serve as its metadata. Although these disparate efforts continue, there are increasing discussions of a cooperative nature to formulate nonspecialized metadata elements that can be more broadly understood and hence more broadly used.

1. General Metadata: Templates, Cores, and Frameworks

There is no clear linear development for metadata, but different initiatives from a variety of disciplines have resulted in efforts to enhance resource retrieval in those arenas, and collaborative work based on broad expertise is underway. Librarians, interested in embracing or merely coping with the emerging "electronic library," have discussed, researched, and written about the potential future for these libraries. Individual libraries, including the

Library of Congress, have work underway to collect and make available electronic resources. Overall, this work emphasizes the need for effective descriptions, perhaps in the form of metadata, for these electronic resources.

General metadata structures have been proposed or developed within and outside the library community. The IAFA templates were developed by the IETF Working Group on Internet Anonymous FTP Archives (IAFA) for use with resources on anonymous FTP sites (Dempsey and Weibel, 1996). There are a number of different template types, such as: SITEINFO, USER, DOCUMENT, IMAGE, SOFTWARE, USENET, VIDEO, FAQ, and others (Beckett, 1995). The templates permit use of numerous elements, including title, author, source, citation, publisher, creation date, last revision date, version size, language, ISBN, ISSN, copyright, and keywords, etc.[10] Beckett (1995) describes how these templates can be implemented, with some modification, "in a real archive to store the metadata of lots of different types of documents and software and to derive WWW, gopher and text indices from them." In his implementation, content for some elements was automatically provided and so could then be automatically updated, while other content was added by the administrator.

The ROADS (Resource Organisation and Discovery in Subject-Based Services) development project in the Access to Network Resources area of the United Kingdom's eLib (Electronic Libraries Progamme) chose to use the IAFA templates as the foundation for its metadata structure because they were text based and human readable and because of the simple record structure that encourages descriptions from authors and others (Heery, 1996). The project requires "a description which is simple to create yet full enough for effective retrieval and relevance. . . . ROADS is looking at IAFA/WHOIS++ templates because they offer a basis for international consensus and because we can influence their development" (Dempsey, 1996; Osborne, 1996). The Centre for Earth Observation (CEO) in Italy also uses the IAFA templates, and they are collaborating in The URN Interoperability Project (TURNIP) (Iannella, 1996).

Another more general metadata format is proposed for bibliographic records describing technical reports (RFC1807) (Lasher and Cohen, 1995). The format was developed by computer specialists and librarians for use in the Networked Computer Science Technical Report Library (NCSTRL) project to exchange bibliographic records for technical reports. The authors consider the format to be simple, with easy to read alphabetic tags that may

[10] Palowitch and Horowitz (1996, pp. 117–118) list 27 elements as examples of those contained in IAFA Templates, including: Template-type; Category; Title; URI; Short-title; Author; Admin; Source; Requirements; Description; Bibliography; Citation; Publication-status; Publisher; Copyright; Creation-Date; Discussion; Keywords; Version; Format; Size; Language; Character-Set; ISBN; ISSN; Last-Revision-Date; Library-Catalog.

serve as a link in digital libraries "between the physical world of scientific works and the on-line world of digital objects."[11] RFC1807 includes 28 elements, again, many familiar: title, author, revision, date, pages, copyright, keyword, etc., and some specialized to this particular use, for example, contract number, grant number, etc. As noted above, implementation of this format is within the NCSTRL institutions.

While both of these are fairly general, they were created with specific needs in mind as the respective sets of elements reflect. Also, it seems clear that the number, more than 20 in each case, the detail, and naming of elements is such that some expertise would be needed for implementation, and though some elements might be system generated, overall these would be too extensive to be used by the broad spectrum of individuals posting information to the Internet.

Another proposed metadata standard grew out of the OCLC/NCSA (National Center for Supercomputing Applications) Metadata Workshop in March, 1995.[12] The workshop was convened to explore options for developing resource description records (metadata) that were intended to be more informative than existing basic index access, but less complete (and hence less time consuming to create) than a formal cataloging record. The workshop included a variety of participants ranging from librarians and archivists, to computer and information scientists, to members of the Internet Engineering Task Force (IETF). Although there was a diversity of background and approach, the participants all agreed that any standard metadata set would be better than none (Caplan and Guenther, 1996). The output from the workshop was the Dublin Metadata Core Element Set, 13 elements that could be used to "facilitate the discovery of document-like objects in a networked environment such as the Internet" (Weibel, 1995a).

The Dublin Core is centered around the following principles: intrisicality (properties of the work that could be discovered based on the work in hand), extensibility (proposed elements could be augmented by additional data as required by objects not adequately described by core elements), syntax independence (to avoid specific syntactic links so as to make the elements more widely useable), optionality (all elements are optional), repeatability (all elements are repeatable), and modifiability (elements can be modified by inclusion of a qualifier) (Weibel, 1995a). The Dublin Core Elements as established

[11] RFC1807 fields include: Bib-Version; ID; Entry date; Organization; Title; Type; Revision; Withdraw; Author; Corp-author; Contact for the author(s); Date of publication; Pages count; Copyright, permissions and disclaimers; Handle; Other_access; Retrieval; Keyword; Cr-category; Period; Series; Monitoring organization(s); Funding organization(s); Grant number(s); Language name; Notes; Abstract; End (Lasher and Cohen, 1995).

[12] OCLC/NCSA Metadata Workshop. Available: http://www.oclc.org:5047/oclc/research/conferences/metadata/metadata.html

in 1995 consisted of: Subject, Title, Author, Publisher, OtherAgent, Date, ObjectType, (genre), Form (physical manifestation), Identifier (string or number used to uniquely identify the object), Relation (to other objects), Source (objects from which it is derived), Language, and Coverage (spatial location and temporal durations) (Weibel, 1995a). In fact, the element set is not unlike a brief, but in some ways enhanced, cataloging record. Brugger suggests that the Dublin Core is "unsatisfactory" because it includes only a subset of those fields required by AACR2 rather than examining more closely what "creators of digital libraries have said they want to distribute and/or what creators of networked objects are capable of providing" (Brugger, 1996, p. 72). She notes, however, that it is syntax independent and suggests that with necessary management data included "users of networked information objects would benefit from a quantum leap in the level of their empowerment" (Brugger, 1996, p. 72).

But the Dublin Core was designed to complement other resource descriptions, those that might be automatically generated, as well as those that require more time intensive creation, such as traditional cataloging records. "Records created from the Dublin Core are intended to mediate these extremes, affording a simple structured record that may be enhanced or mapped to more complex records as called for, either by direct extension or by a link to a more elaborate record" (Weibel, *et al.*, 1995). If commonly accepted, this data element set could be promoted for used by authors and publishers alike to provide metadata for and within their original works. Perhaps implemented through inclusion of appropriate templates in authoring or publishing tools, the Dublin Core could serve as the basis for more detailed cataloging or as a link to more specific descriptions required in particular disciplines, not replacing them but facilitating access to them, and become a standard that could be easily understood by a variety of end users (Dempsey and Weibel, 1996).

While work continues on the Dublin Core, several projects are beginning to include its elements in at least experimental ways. OCLC is incorporating it in its ongoing work with their SPECTRUM project that "presents an interface to users who wish to register and describe a resource for inclusion in a Web-accessible database of Internet resources, where this description is built on the Dublin Core" (Godby and Miller, 1996). TURNIP, which was begun by the Distributed Systems Technology Centre in Australia, has chosen the Dublin Core as its metadata scheme (Iannella, 1996). The Dublin Core is to be tested as well in the Nordic Metadata Project to create "a Nordic Metadata production, indexing and retrieval environment" to facilitate interchange of digital documents within Scandinavia (Hakala, 1996). The National Document and Information Service (NDIS), a joint project of the national libraries of Australia and New Zealand, reports use of the Dublin Core as a basic structure of bibliographic data, one they are expanding as they proceed (Pearce, 1996).

Developers of the Dublin Core were aware that much was still needed for its implementation, since the Dublin Core was merely a list of categories presented in commonly understood terminology, a data structure, not a delivery system. And just as a written text does not often sit independently, but may be complemented by a title page (and its verso), an index or table of contents, a book review, a revised or abridged version, or an analytical critique, an electronic resource would not be described solely by metadata such as the Dublin Core, but would need to be accompanied by additional information, more specialized descriptions about revisions, file structure, source, technical data needed to use the file, or a way to access these data. This awareness that additional work was needed prior to full implementation led to another workshop a year later when again a diverse group met to further develop the concept of the Dublin Core to identify and resolve "impediments to deployment of a Dublin Core style record for resource description" (Dempsey and Weibel, 1996).

The OCLC/UKOLN (United Kingdom Office for Library and Information Networking) Warwick Metadata Workshop was held in Warwick, England, in April, 1996 and very quickly the focus of this workshop became "extensibility."[13] Attendees built on the Dublin Core and developed a proposal for a container architecture to be known as the Warwick Framework. They proposed a modular framework that would allow a resource to be accompanied by a variety of other metadata sets. The framework would be "extensible, to allow for new metadata types; distributed, to allow external metadata objects to be referenced; recursive, to allow metadata objects to be treated as 'information content' and have metadata objects associated with them" (Dempsey and Weibel, 1996). The Warwick Framework would provide a means of "aggregating logically, and perhaps concretely (through the use of specific data structure) distinct packages of metadata" (Lagoze, *et al.*, 1996). A framework structure could accommodate a variety of separately maintained metadata and so could more easily serve a diverse community of users (Dempsey and Weibel, 1996). For example, a single electronic resource might be accompanied by a simple metadata set such as the Dublin Core, but might also include a traditional cataloging record, a content rating (PICS, Platform for Internet Content Selection), information on the terms and conditions for use of the resource, provenance, linkage or relationship data, or structural data (Lagoze *et al.*, 1996).

These authors (Lagoze *et al.*, 1996) also present some possible implementations of the Warwick Framework based on work now underway. Proposals

[13]OCLC/UKOLN Metadata Conference. Available: http://www.oclc.org:5047/oclc/research/conferences/metadata2/metadata.html

are in development for incorporation of the Warwick Framework using HTML (HyperText Markup Language, an SGML application), MIME (Multipurpose Internet Multimedia Extensions), and SGML (Standard Generalized Markup Language). The first, inclusion of metadata in HTML, is particularly useful, as HTML is used broadly in Web documents. Weibel (1996c) reports on discussions at the 1996 World Wide Web Conference, Distributed Indexing and Searching Workshop that resulted in a proposed convention on embedding structured metadata within HTML documents.

The first two OCLC metadata workshops focused primarily on textual "document-like objects," but in September, 1996, OCLC and the Coalition for Networked Information (CNI) held the CNI/OCLC Workshop on Metadata for Networked Images[14] to discuss the requirements of networked images and imagebases with regard to this basic set of metadata elements. Seventy individuals involved in networked image description explored the need and desirability to expand the Dublin Core metadata element set for images. The preliminary report of the workshop indicated consensus among participants that "the Dublin Core, within the context of the Warwick Framework, affords a foundation for the development of a simple resource description model to support network based discovery of static images (items or collections of items, online or offline)" (Weibel, 1996b). The group recommended, however, that some refinements to the original Dublin Core were needed.

Discussions following the meeting among previous workshop attendees resulted in the following revised draft of a 15-element Dublin Core: Title, Creator (Author or Creator), Subject (Subject or Keywords), Description (textual description of the contents of the resource), Publisher, Contributors, Date, Type (Resource Type, e.g., home page, poem, technical report), Format (e.g., text/html, ASCII), Identifier (Resource Identified, e.g., URL, ISBN), Source (work from which the resource was derived), Language, Relation (e.g., item in a collection, chapter in a book), Coverage (spatial locations and temporal durations), and Rights (e.g., link to copyright notice or rights management statement) (Weibel, 1996d). The two added elements are Description and Rights, although for several others the term used was somewhat altered (i.e., Author became Creator; ObjectType became Type; OtherAgent became Contributors; Form became Format).

The possibility of using general metadata schemes such as the Dublin Core as the foundation for traditional cataloging, or the ability, given the syntax independence of the Dublin Core, of simply defining its elements in USMARC terms has led to exercises in mapping the Dublin Core to MARC. By comparing elements and fields of each it is possible to determine the functionality of the match. Caplan and Guenther (1996) comment on this

[14] CNI/OCLC Image Metadata Workshop. Available: http://www.oclc.org:5046/conferences/imagemeta/index.html.

type of mapping and anticipate that problems might arise in determining which USMARC fields to map to since for some elements there would be several possibilities, as for author, title, subject, identifying number, relationships, for example. The authors also question if a mechanical mapping from the Dublin Core to USMARC would be necessary, for although supplied metadata might possibly be helpful in describing the resource, items are cataloged on a one by one basis and a cataloger's experience and subjectivity would certainly affect the selection of which fields to use and what the content of those fields might be. Moving from a simple to complex form would require manual augmentation of the record. A discussion paper presented to MARBI[15] in 1995 provides a preliminary view of how this mapping might work; this work has been updated, and another discussion paper is forthcoming (Library of Congress, 1995a; Guenther, 1996).

2. Specialized Metadata: TEI, EAD, and FGDC Standards

In addition to more generalized metadata, librarians and subject specialists in a variety of fields have undertaken development of specialized metadata sets. Three are presented here.

In the late 1940s humanities scholars began to use electronic texts in their research, with such use evolving as computers changed, but it was hypertext systems that offered these scholars more flexibility than ever before. Hockey (1994) presents a concise overview of these developments and the need to devise a way to mark these texts to make them more useful now and in the future. In 1987 planning began to create guidelines for encoding electronic texts through a project called the Text Encoding Initiative (TEI).[16] Standard Generalized Markup Language (SGML), approved as an internationally recognized standard in 1986, was considered a good basis for the encoding and interchange of electronic texts through the TEI scheme (Gaynor, 1994; Hockey, 1996). "SGML provides a way of encoding electronic texts that is independent of any particular computer hardware or software. It consists of plain ASCII files with markup tags embedded in the text that are themselves ASCII characters. The principle of SGML is descriptive, not prescriptive" (Hockey, 1996, p. 6; TEI, 1996).

Among the many elements in the TEI scheme is the TEI "header." It is incorporated as part of the electronic resource and may serve as a chief source of information much as a title page does for a printed book. It is parallel in many ways to metadata as it provides a description of the file to come and the basic information needed to use it (Hockey, 1996, p. 7). More

[15] MARBI (Machine-Readable Bibliographic Information) is the American Library Association's interdivisional committee that reviews and recommends standards in machine-readable forms of bibliographic information.

[16] Electronic Text Encoding Interchange. Available: http://etext.virginia.edu/TEI.html.

specifically, the TEI header includes: (1) file description with full bibliographical description; (2) encoding description which presents the relationship between the electronic text and its source; (3) a text profile which presents the subject of the file and production information, and notes individuals who may have had responsibility for producing the file; and (4) a revision history (Giordano, 1994). Gaynor (1994) proposes that the TEI header presents librarians the opportunity to expand traditional approaches to cataloging by allowing them to imbed a cataloging record within an electronic resource (Gaynor, 1994). Additionally, Hockey (1996) observes that elements in the TEI header can be mapped into the USMARC record and so be used as a source for catalogers. "The TEI header represents the first systematic attempt to document an electronic text file. It is designed for use by catalogers and software developers as well as the end users of the text" (Hockey, 1996, p. 9). Creation of an Standard Generalized Markup Language (SGML) Document Type Definition (DTD) for the MARC record is in process and will map MARC and SGML (Davis-Brown and Williamson, 1996). Since the TEI was designed to enhance communication of information, a number of institutions have implemented it in their work with electronic texts, among them the University of Virginia Library's Electronic Text Center, established in 1992 (Gaynor, 1994), and the Center for Electronic Texts in the Humanities of Rutgers and Princeton Universities (Hockey, 1994).

More recently archivists also have developed a type of "metadata," contained in the Encoded Archival Description/Document Type Definition (EAD DTD).[17] With the growth of the Internet and the Web, archivists sought to expand access to their holdings by making archival finding aids more widely available. In 1993, the University of California at Berkeley began a project to "investigate the desirability and feasibility of developing an encoding standard for machine readable finding aids" (Library of Congress, 1996b). With this goal in mind, individuals from the Society of American Archivists, the Library of Congress, OCLC, and the Research Libraries Group cooperated to develop standards and by 1995 had completed a draft of the EAD. Like the TEI, it is a "nonproprietary" encoding standard, and it too is an SGML application.

Archivists wanted to include information for archival materials in addition to what was in the more traditional cataloging record. As a result, the EAD consists of two segments: the first a header, with information about the finding aid itself (title, compiler, date), and the second a segment that includes information about the collection, record group, or series. TEI conventions and guidelines were followed as appropriate. The aim was to create a standard and guidelines that could be implemented by individuals little acquainted

[17] Encoded Archival Description (EAD). Available: http://lcweb.loc.gov/loc/standards/ead/.

with SGML. "With respect to USMARC, the encoding standard recognizes the interrelationship between catalog records and finding aids and it provides for the use of a MARC equivalency attribute for those finding aid elements matching USMARC fields" (Ann Arbor Accords, 1996).

In addition to the work at the University of California at Berkeley, Harvard University, in its Harvard/Radcliffe Digital Finding Aids Project (DFAP), has based its own guidelines on the EAD (Harvard University, 1996). The Library of Congress was one of the first libraries to implement the EAD standard when placing its online registers of their archival collections on the World Wide Web (Davis-Brown and Williamson, 1996). The Library of Congress will also serve as the "maintenance agency" for the EAD. The EAD was in beta testing in mid-1996, and training in EAD application is scheduled during the coming year.

The presentation of geospatial information has changed dramatically in only a relatively few years moving from the traditional and very familiar paper map to massive digital files and complex computerized systems. Based on work to establish a national clearing house to aid in collecting and accessing digital spatial data, the Federal Geographic Data Committee (FGDC) worked to establish and implement metadata standards and mandated that after January, 1995, Federal agencies would use these standards on newly created geospatial data.[18] The FGDC promotes the "value" of geospatial metadata: "The concept of metadata is familiar to most people who deal with spatial issues. A map legend is pure metadata. . . . Metadata are simply that type of descriptive information applied to a digital geospatial file. They're a common set of terms and definitions to use when documenting geospatial data" (FGDC, 1995, p. 12).

The standard includes the following information: availability, including data that would allow users to know if data exist for a particular geographic location; fitness for use (will the data meet the users needs?); access, including what users need to know to acquire the data; and transfer, including the information required to process and use the data (Domaratz, 1996). Content of metadata is specified, allowing flexibility for implementation. The 1994 Content Standards for Digital Geospatial Metadata (CSDGM) indicates that metadata contain "data about the content, quality, condition, and other characteristics of data" (FGDC, 1994, p. 1). The metadata elements listed are: Identification Information; with the subelements Data Quality Information, Spatial Data Organization Information, Entity and Attribute Information, Distribution Information; followed by Metadata Reference Information, with the subelements Metadata Date, Metadata Contact, Metadata Standard Name, Metadata Standard Version, Metadata Access Constraints, Metadata

[18] FGDC's CSDGM. Available: http://geochange.er.usgs.gov/pub/tools/metadata/standard/metadata.html

Use Constraints, and Metadata Security Information. Each element in this standard is explicitly defined in the 1994 document (FGDC, 1994). The CSDGM has been mapped to MARC, and this has led to modifications in MARC that incorporate elements for specialized geospatial information (Library of Congress, 1996e).

The Alexandria Project at the University of California and Santa Barbara utilizes these standards along with USMARC standards in their digital library, the Alexandria Digital Library (ADL). This "library" was developed as part of the National Science Foundation-funded Digital Library Initiative to investigate the problems of a distributed digital library for geographically referenced information and to build a testbed system as basis for an operational library (Frew *et al.*, 1996). "The ADL will give users Internet access to and allow information extraction from broad classes of geographically referenced materials. In this case, having access means being able to browse, view, and download data and metadata. Information extraction involves the application of local or remote procedures to selected data and metadata" (Smith, 1996, p. 54). The combined use of USMARC and FGDC standards, resulting in a total of some 350 fields, has allowed cataloging of spatial data, including "remote-sensing imagery, digitized maps, digital raster and vector data sets, text, videos, and remote WWW servers" (Smith, 1996, p. 55) and provides a hands-on foundation for the use of this metadata in a digital library, as staff identify, catalog, and so create descriptions for these collections.

V. Moving toward a Digital Library

As libraries incorporate greater numbers of electronic resources into their library collections they must simultaneously seek to reexamine what defines a library and how they might select, access, manage, and preserve these resources. Metadata is but one small component in this effort, but it is important to focus on the whole as well as the individual parts. In the United States, through activities supported by the Coalition for Networked Information, the National Science Foundation, the Library of Congress, the American Library Association, and individual libraries and librarians across the country, we are gaining a greater understanding of this digital library.

The Coalition for Networked Information was formed by the Association of Research Libraries, CAUSE, and EDUCOM in 1990 to "promote the creation of and access to information resources in networked environments in order to enrich scholarship and to enhance intellectual productivity" (Coalition for Networked Information, 1997). The Coalition seeks "to inspire . . . to inform . . . to influence . . . [and] to synergize" (Coalition for Networked Information, 1997). These goals are met in part through the work of its Task Force of institutions and organizations representing a broad spectrum from the world of information management. Meeting twice each year, Task Force members share information on research in progress and initiatives under development relating to information resources in networked environments through presentations, project briefings, and opportunities for formal and informal discussion.

The potential and challenges of future digital libraries can only be understood through experimentation and research. To further this effort, the National Science Foundation with the Department of Defense Advanced Research Projects Agency and the National Aeronautics and Space Administration funded six research projects in 1994 as part of a Digital Library Initiative. "The project's focus is to dramatically advance the means to collect, store, and organize information in digital forms, and to make it available for searching, retrieval and processing via communication networks—all in user-friendly ways" (Griffin, 1997). Projects funded include: Carnegie Mellon University (Informedia: Integrated Speech, Image and Language Understanding for Creation and Exploration of Digital Video Libraries); University of California at Berkeley (The Environmental Electronic Library: A Prototype of a Scalable, Intelligent, Distributed Electronic Library); the University of Michigan (The University of Michigan Digital Libraries Research Project); The University of Illinois at Urbana-Champaign (Building the Interspace: Digital Library Infrastructure for a University Engineering Community); the University of California at Santa Barbara (The Alexandria Project: Towards a Distributed Digital Library with Comprehensive Services for Images and Spatially Referenced Information); and Stanford University (The Stanford Integrated Digital Library Project) (Griffin, 1997).

The Library of Congress is involved in the National Digital Library Program, where the goal is to "make available on the Internet five million digitized images and texts from the Library's unique collections by the year 2000" (Davis-Brown and Williamson, 1996, pp. 171–172). In addition, the Library has sponsored workshops and seminars on digital topics. The 1994 Seminar on Cataloging Digital Documents addressed the impact of digital information on cataloging, examining how to provide access to electronic texts and other electronic resources (Thomas, 1994). Catalogers, library and information science faculty, and computer scientists and systems administrators met to gain information about ongoing initiatives and discuss how catalogers might deal with digital materials (David-Brown and Williamson, 1996, p.172).

In 1995, the Library hosted the Organizing the Global Digital Library (OGDL) Conference, where participants sought to "form a consensus on a list of principles and assumptions regarding the nature or organization in the digital library of the future" (Library of Congress, 1995b). Among the themes identified in the conference were several related to "organizing for access," including the need to augment cataloging data through human intervention to maximize use of Internet software tools and to find ways to expand the use of metadata that forms part of digital objects (Library of Congress, 1995b).

In May, 1996, Organizing the Global Digital Library II was held at the Library of Congress and served to update participants on developments regarding digital libraries (Library of Congress, 1996g). Among the conference proposals for future work were several dealing with metadata. The need for "real" work was deemed important, and the proposals included working with document creators to generate metadata, building on the Dublin Core to develop metadata guidelines and distribute them for review and comment, examining the role of the TEI in the global digital library, and promoting the use of the EAD (Library of Congress, 1996f).

In the realm of cataloging standards and practice, several groups within the American Library Association's Association for Library Collections & Technical Services (ALCTS) are investigating metadata. ALCTS appointed a Meta Access Task Force (first named the Task Force to Define Bibliographic Access in the Electronic Environment) that was charged: . . . "to lead the way in defining access and bibliographic control mechanisms for information in electronic form and communicating that mechanism to the users of the electronic information" (American Library Association, ALCTS, 1995). In addition, two specially appointed Task Forces of the ALCTS Cataloging and Classification Section, Committee on Cataloging: Description and Access (CC:DA) are looking at different types of metadata. One is examining the Dublin Core and the other the TEI. These groups are to report in early 1997. As noted above, MARBI regularly reviews and evaluates proposed cataloging standards. It is before this body that proposals for the USMARC 856 Field were made and there that discussions of mapping the Dublin Core to MARC are ongoing.

VI. Discussion and Conclusions

It is clear that electronic resources will remain, no matter what form the Web or some newer iteration of it takes. The mass of resources now available includes many that are useful in current research and many too that will be valuable in the future as a documentation of our time and thoughts. But many Internet resources are trivial, ephemeral, or fleeting. We must consider appropriate methods to organize and manage the broad spectrum of these resources, taking into consideration the nature of the Internet and realizing that each method has its strengths and weaknesses, its supporters and detractors. "Given the explosion in available information resources of all types, it remains to be seen whether the majority of users will be better served by simplified access to a wider range of materials, or whether increased access will be useless without more sophisticated and discriminating retrieval capabilities" (Caplan and Guenther, 1996, p. 57).

The experience gained by catalogers around the world indicates that electronic resources may be cataloged using traditional methods. In arguing to give traditional cataloging its chance, Reagor-Flannery (1995) suggests it is important to test current methods in describing electronic resources, noting that "new tools generally are not developed before old tools have been tried and found wanting," and she also stresses that catalogers should play a role in this "cultural transition" to the digital library (Reagor-Flannery, 1995, pp. 214–215). Based on reports from the field, librarians are cataloging electronic resources, and traditional cataloging is found to be an effective means of incorporating specific resources into local online catalogs.

Many consider cataloging standards to be complex and inflexible, as well as incomprehensible to the outsider, particularly the number-based MARC format. But standards can change as seen in the addition of the 856 field for Electronic Location and Access, and while Larsgaard (1996) looks to the potential of automation as an aid to automatically generating digital data, she also suggests that catalogers reexamine and rework cataloging rules so they are more reflective of the many types of materials that will require description. Cataloging is also time consuming, particularly in view of the numbers of uncataloged Internet resources and their volatility, but cataloging carries its strengths into the digital world. In the broader picture, traditional cataloging is part of an integrated approach to information resources that includes selection, organization, maintenance, and preservation. Cataloging is also based on standards that support consistency in the form and selection of "data" in the cataloging record. These value-added aspects of cataloging are important, and Morville (1996) suggests that people will come to recognize and depend on this in an Internet environment. Even lacking traditional cataloging for all the Internet, a foundation in a cataloging approach will benefit information organization. Taylor and Clemson (1996) reinforce this when they state: "We should recognize that it is the *principle* developed especially over the last 150 years that we want to defend and to insist be used by organizers of the Internet, not an undying affection for AACR2 per se. Standards of description assure built-in predictability and eliminate most duplication by analyzing the linkages between entities." They add that for Internet documents of lasting value, traditional cataloging principles should be applied. The need to catalog electronic resources, particularly those of local importance, would exist whether or not metadata accompanied the resources.

While traditional cataloging may be unnecessary for the larger mass of materials on the Web, a quick-to-implement description in the form of metadata may be feasible. Metadata accompanied by technological advances have the potential to more easily attack and control the massive number of resources on the Internet. If metadata were based on a foundation of effective standards, it might fill the information–organization void, for a metadata approach to resource description has many advantages. Certainly, if metadata were autogenerated and system supplied, it would lessen the need for human intervention and might well assure timely completion of minimal descriptions. Data supplied by an author or creator to a template-type section of resource software would also assure provision of at least minimum information at the earliest possible moment, presumably by those most familiar with the resource. If applied according to basic standards, this metadata might greatly enhance current search or "surfing" methods on the Internet. However, automatic generation of data will be self-limited, and individuals creating metadata sets for their own resources may lack an understanding of the finer points of description or be unaware of the importance of their work to the overall retrieval/discovery of electronic resources. Metadata initiatives remain under development with many issues still unresolved. How will metadata be updated as part of a dynamic and frequently changed resource? Will metadata describe collections of resources, single resources, or both? These new approaches to "cataloging" or resource description are more open than US-MARC format standards, but Mandel and Wolven also point out that these records will lack "name collocation, subject access, version control and genre identification" (Mandel and Wolven, 1996, p. 40). Any implementation of metadata in electronic resources, particularly if it is to depend on resource creators, will reflect different levels of use, understanding, and implementation. Efforts to "tame" the Internet cannot wait for a time when all issues might be resolved, for even minimal implementation might afford needed control and serve to enhance Internet access.

Computer experts are constantly working to improve and change our use and approach to the Internet, so "it is not unreasonable to think that the possibilities for finding information stored in computers are much more sophisticated and user friendly than anything offered by libraries. There is every reason to look forward to the virtual world which computers can make possible" (Franchet, 1993, p. 10). But Franchet (1993) also acknowledges the need for standardized metadata and precisely defined descriptive elements and classifications. Work underway with metadata sets such as the Dublin Core, which is syntax independent and clearly named, could provide a "semantic interoperability" among record types and serve as the basic description for resource discovery (Weibel, 1996a).

Beyond directing Internet "explorers" toward needed resources, metadata may also provide the basis for more complete and complex cataloging records (Xu, 1996; Mandel and Wolven, 1996). Although some see an automated conversion of metadata from standard to standard, others question the effectiveness of moving simplistic data to more complex descriptions such as a catalog record, since additional information would need to be added or existing information verified (e.g., authority control) through human intervention (Caplan and Guenther, 1996; Xu, 1996). However, this future use of automation and transfer of data from one data standard to another would "multiply the effects of a feasible investment of human intellectual effort by supplementing it with software aimed at achieving principles of good access" (Mandel and Wolven, 1996, p. 40).

Through a blending of computer power, computer expertise, and information organization fundamentals the Internet may become tamed, at least to the point where there is a reasonable expectation of locating and returning to desired information in a timely and dependable fashion. Great progress has been made through cooperative efforts to establish metadata standards, and the efficacy of these proposed standards is being tested worldwide. But implementation of metadata is only part of the process, for along with this involvement in information organization and standards the librarian brings an awareness to the process of the greater realm of resource management. Librarians must be involved in the world of electronic resources, for "only then will the distribution of those materials to local and remote users be guaranteed to be comprehensive, enduring, integrated, and of consistently high quality" (Sha, *et al.*, 1996).

Butterfield (1996) notes the similarity of today's problems in coping with Internet "publishing" to those encountered in the early days of printing. "We are grappling with an emerging and mutable publication medium for which we have few definitive answers because we have not discovered all of the questions yet." We are discovering those questions and answering them, only to be faced with new ones. Traditional cataloging will undoubtedly continue to play a vital role in describing substantial electronic resources available on the Internet, particularly those selected as important for local audiences. But, like the past, the future will not depend on a single method for describing, accessing, or organizing information resources. Metadata is but a small part of Internet access. Developed carefully and broadly but with timely implementation it might both assist computer facilitated searching and serve as the basis of traditional cataloging records. It may become the middle ground between simple and complex, general and detailed resource description. In the future when searching the Internet for the term "metadata" perhaps the computer will respond:"You have found 326 relevant documents from a total of 213,325,685 indexed Web pages, and based on your research interests, our in-depth conversations, and your specific inquiry, they should be exactly what you need. Please let me know if you have additional questions."

References

American Library Association (ALA), Association for Library Collections and Technical Services (ALCTS) (1995). ALCTS Task Force on Meta Access: ALCTS taskforce charge. Available: http://www.lib.virginia.edu/alcts/about/charge.html.

American Library Association (ALA), Resources and Technical Services Division, Cataloging and Classification Section, Committee on Cataloging: Description and Access (1984). *Guidelines for Using AACR2, Chapter 9 for Cataloging Microcomputer Software.* ALA, Chicago.

Ann Arbor accords: Principles and criteria for an SGML document type definition (DTD) for finding aids (1996). Available: http://sunsite.berkeley.edu/FindingAids/EAD/accords.html.

Beckett, D. (1995). IAFA templates in use as Internet metadata. Available: http://www.w3.org/pub/Conferences/WWW4/Papers/52/.

Brugger, J. M. (1996). Cataloging for digital libraries. *Cataloging and Classification Quarterly* **22**(3/4), 59–73.

Butterfield, K. L. (1996). Catalogers and the creation of metadata systems: A collaborative vision at the University of Michigan. Available: http://www.oclc.org/oclc/man/colloq/butter.htm.

Cammarata, S., Kameny, I., Lender, J., and Replogle, C. (1994). A metadata management system to support data interoperability, reuse and sharing. *Journal of Database Management* **5**(2), 30–40.

Caplan, P., and Guenther, R. (1996). Metadata for Internet resources: The Dublin Core metadata elements set and its mapping to USMARC. *Cataloging and Classification Quarterly* **22**(3/4), 43–58.

Coalition for Networked Information (1997). Coalition for Networked Information. Available: http://www.cni.org/docs/CNI.html.

Davis-Brown, B., and Williamson, D. (1996). Cataloging at the Library of Congress in the digital age. *Cataloging and Classification Quarterly* **22**(3/4), 171–196.

Dempsey, L. (1996). ROADS to desire: Some UK and other European metadata and resource discovery projects. *D-Lib Magazine*, July/August. Available: http://www.dlib.org/dlib/july96/07dempsey.html.

Dempsey, L., and Weibel, S. L. (1996). The Warwick Metadata Workshop: A framework for the deployment of resource description. *D-Lib Magazine*, July/August. Available: http://www.dlib.org/dlib/july96/07weibel.html.

Diamond, E., and Bates, S. (1995). The ancient history of the Internet. *American Heritage* **46**(6), 34–36, 38, 40, 42, 44–45.

Dillon, M., and Jul, E. (1996). Cataloging Internet resources: The convergence of libraries and Internet resources. *Cataloging and Classification Quarterly* **22**(3/4), 197–238.

Dillon, M., Jul, E., Burge, M., and Hickey, C. (1993). *Assessing Information on the Internet: Toward Providing Library Services for Computer-Mediated Communication.* OCLC Online Computer Library Center, Dublin, OH.

Dodd, S. A., and Sandberg-Fox, A. M. (1985). *Cataloging Microcomputer Files: A Manual of Interpretation for AACR2.* American Library Association, Chicago.

Domaratz, M. (1996). Finding and accessing spatial data in the national spatial data infrastructure. In *Geographic Information Systems and Libraries: Patrons, Maps, and Spatial Information* (L. C. Smith and M. Gluck, eds.), pp. 31–40. Clinic on Library Applications of Data Processing, 1995, Graduate School of Library and Information Science, University of Illinois, Urbana-Champaign.

Erway, R. L. (1996). Digital initiatives of the Research Libraries Group. *D-Lib Magazine*, December. Available: http://www.dlib.org/dlib/december96/rlg/12erway.html.

Federal Geographic Data Committee (1994). *Content Standards for Digital Geospatial Metadata.* FGDC, Reston, VA.

Federal Geographic Data Committee (1995). *The Value of Metadata.* FGDC, Reston, VA.

Floridi, L. (1996). The Internet: Which future for organised knowledge, Frankenstein or Pygmalion? Pt. 1. Pt. 2. *Electronic Library* **14**(1), 43–48, 49–52.

Franchet, Y. (1993). Metadata and official statistics. In *Statistical Meta Information Systems: Proceedings of the Conference, Luxembourg, 2 to 4 February 1993*, pp. 9–12. Office for Official Publications of the European Communities, Luxembourg.

Frew, J., Freeston, M., Kemp, R. B., Simpson, J., Smith, T., Wells, A., and Zheng, Q. (1996). The Alexandria digital library testbed. *D-Lib Magazine*, July/August. Available: http://www.dlib.org/dlib/july96/alexandria/07frew.html.

Gaynor, E. (1994). Cataloging electronic texts: The University of Virginia library experience. *Library Resources and Technical Services* **38**(4), 403–413.

Giordano, R. (1994). The documentation of electronic texts using text encoding initiative headers: An introduction. *Library Resources and Technical Services* **38**(4), 389–401.

Godby, J., and Miller, E. (1996). A metalanguage for describing Internet resources using the Dublin Core element set. Available: http://www.uni-freiburg.de/rz/inet96/a2/a2__2.htm.

Gorman, M., and Winkler, P. W., eds. (1978). *Anglo-American Cataloguing Rules*, 2nd ed. Prepared by the American Library Association, The British Library, The Canadian Committee on Cataloguing, the Library Association, the Library of Congress. American Library Association, Chicago.

Gorman, M., and Winkler, P. W., eds. (1988). *Anglo-American Cataloging Rules.* 2nd rev. ed. Prepared under the direction of the Joint Steering Committee for Revision of AACR. Canadian Library Association, Ottawa.

Griffin, S. M. (1997). NSF/DARPA/NASA digital libraries initiative projects. Available: http://www.cise.nsf.gov/iris/DLHome.html.

Guenther, R. C. (1996). Dublin Core/MARC crosswalk. 19 December. Available E-mail: META2@mrrl.lut.ac.uk. Also available: http://www.roads.lut.ac.uk/lists/meta2/0568.html.

Hakala, J. (1996). Description of the Nordic metadata project: Cataloguing, indexing and retrieval of digital documents. Available: http://linnea.helsinki.fi/meta/projplan.html.

Hakala, J., Husby, O., and Koch, T. (1996). Warwick Framework and Dublin Core set provide a comprehensive infrastructure for network resource description. Available: http://www.ub2.lu.se/tk/warwick.html.

Harris, M. H. (1995). *History of Libraries in the Western World*, 4th ed. Scarecrow Press, Metuchen, NJ.

Harvard University (1996). Harvard/Radcliffe digital finding aids project. Available: http://hul.harvard.edu/dfap.

Heery, R. (1996). ROADS: Resource organisation and discovery in subject-based services. *Ariadne*, Issue 3, May. Available: http://bubl.bath.ac.uk/ariadne/issue3/roads/.

Hockey, S. (1994). Electronic texts in the humanities: A coming of age. In *Literary Texts in an Electronic Age: Scholarly Implications and Library Services* (B. Sutton, ed.), pp. 21–34. Graduate School of Library and Information Science, University of Illinois, Urbana-Champaign.

Hockey, S. (1996). Creating and using electronic editions. In *The Literary Text in the Digital Age* (R.J. Finneran, ed.), pp. 1–21. University of Michigan Press, Ann Arbor.

Hoogcarspel, A. (1994). *Guidelines for Cataloging Monographic Electronic Texts at the Center for Electronic Texts in the Humanities*, CETH Tech. Rep. No. 1. Center for Electronic Texts in the Humanities, Rutgers and Princeton Universities, New Brunswick, NJ.

Hudgins-Bonafield, C. (1995). Who will master metadata? *Network Computing* **6**(8), 102–104, 106–108.

Iannella, R. (1996). TURNIP: The URN interoperability project. *D-Lib Magazine*, March. Available: http://www.dlib.org/dlib/march96/briefings/03turnip.html.

Inmon, W. H. (1992). *Building the Data Warehouse.* QED Technical Publishing Group, Boston.

Jul, E. (1992). Internet resources project volunteers provide critical support. *OCLC Newsletter* **198,** 18–19.

Kramer, S. N., and the editors of Time-Life Books (1967). *Cradle of Civilization.* Time Incorporated, New York.

Lagoze, C., Lynch, C. A., and Daniel, R., Jr. (1996). The Warwick Framework: A container architecture for aggregating sets of metadata. July 12, 1996. Available: http://cs-tr.cs.cornell.edu/Dienst/Repository/2.0/Body/ncstrl.cornell%2fTR96-1593/html.

Larsgaard, M. L. (1996). Cataloging planetospatial data in digital form: old wine, new bottles—new wine, old bottles. In *Geographic Information Systems and Libraries: Patrons, Maps, and Spatial Information* (L. C. Smith and M. Gluck, eds.), pp. 17–30. Clinic on Library Applications of Data Processing, 1995, Graduate School of Library and Information Science, University of Illinois, Urbana-Champaign.

Lasher, R., and Cohen, D. (1995). RFC1807: A format for bibliographic records. Available: http://www.cis.ohio-state.edu/htbin/rfc/rfc1807.html.

Library of Congress (1995a). Mapping the Dublin Core metadata elements to USMARC. May 5, 1995. Discuss. Pap. No.: 86. Available: gopher://marvel.loc.gov:70/00/.listarch/usmarc/dp86.cov.

Library of Congress (1995b). Organizing the global digital library conference. December 11, 1995. Available: gopher://marvel.loc.gov/00/loc/conf.meet/gdl.

Library of Congress (1996a). 25 questions most frequently asked by visitors of the Library of Congress. Available: gopher://marvel.loc.gov/00/loc/facil/25.faqs.

Library of Congress (1996b). EAD finding aid pilot project. Available: http://lcweb2.loc.gov/ammem/ead/.

Library of Congress (1996c). Guidelines for the use of field 856. Rev. March 1996. Available: http://lcweb.loc.gov/marc/856/guide.html.

Library of Congress (1996d). Intercat. Available: http://lcweb.loc.gov/catdir/odgl2/intercat.html.

Library of Congress (1996e). MARC and its relevance in the digital world. Available: http://lcweb.loc.gov/catdir/ogdl2/marc.html.

Library of Congress (1996f). Next steps. Available: http://lcweb.loc.gov/catdir/ogdl2/next.html.

Library of Congress (1996g). Organizing the global digital library II (OGDL II). Available: http://lcweb.loc.gov/catdir/ogdl2/.

Lide, D. R. (1995). Metadata: A description. *Library Hi-Tech* Issues **49–50**(13:1–2), 33-34.

Madsen, M. S., Fogg, I., and Ruggles, C. (1994). Metadata systems: Integrative information technologies. *Libri* **44**(3), 237–257.

Mandel, C. A., and Wolven, R. (1996). Intellectual access to digital documents: Joining proven principles with new technologies. *Cataloging and Classification Quarterly* **22**(3/4), 25–42.

Morville, P. (1996). Revenge of the librarians. *Web Review,* May 10. Available: http://www.webreview.com/96/05/10/webarch/index.html.

Neuss, C., and Kent, R. E. (1995). Conceptual analysis of resource meta-information. *Computer Networks and ISDN Systems* **27,** 973–984.

Notess, G. R. (1996). Internet 'onesearch' with the mega search engines. *Online* **20**(6), 36–39.

OCLC (1994). OCLC: Building a catalog of Internet-accessible materials. Available: http://www.oclc.org/oclc/man/catproj/overview.html.

OCLC (1996). OCLC: Proceedings of the OCLC Internet cataloging colloquium. Available: http://www.oclc.org/oclc/man/colloq/toc.htm.

Olson, N. B., ed. (1995). Cataloging Internet resources: A manual and practical guide. Available: http://www.oclc.org:80/oclc/man/9256cat/toc.htm.

Osborne, C., (1996). ROADS: Further details. Available: http://ukoln.bath.ac.uk/details.html.

Palowitch, C., and Horowitz, L. (1996). Meta-information structures for networked information resources. *Cataloging and Classification Quarterly* **21**(3/4), 109–130.

Pearce, J. (1996). Sidebar: A report from the field. *Library Hi-Tech* **53**(14:1), 9.

Pfaffenberger, B. (1995). *QUE's Computer & Internet Dictionary*. 6th ed. QUE, Indianapolis, IN.

Reagor-Flannery, M. (1995). Cataloging Internet resources. *Bulletin of the Medical Library Association* **83**(2), 211–215.

Scoville, R. (1996). Find it on the net. *PC World* **14**(1), 125-130.

Sha, V. T., Patrick, T. B., and Kochtanek, T. R. (1996). The traditional library and the national information infrastructure. Available: http://www.oclc.org/oclc/man/colloq/sha.htm.

Smith, T. R. (1996). A digital library for geographically referenced materials. *Computer* **29**(5), 54–60.

Taylor, A. G., and Clemson, P. (1996). Access to networked documents: Catalogs? Search engines? Both? Available: http://www.oclc.org/oclc/man/colloq/taylor.htm.

TEI guidelines for electronic text encoding and interchange (1996). Available: http://etext.virginia.edu/TEI.html.

Thomas, S. E. (1994). Summary: Seminar on cataloging digital documents. Available: http://lcweb.loc.gov/catdir/semdigdocs/summary.html.

Weibel, S. (1995a). Metadata: The foundations of resource description. *D-Lib Magazine*, July. Available: http://www.dlib.org/dlib/July95/07weibel.html.

Weibel, S. (1995b). Trends in the world wide web development: May 1995. *Library Hi-Tech*. **51**(13:3), 7–10.

Weibel, S. (1996a). The changing landscape of networked resource description. *Library Hi-Tech* Issue **53**(14:1), 7–10.

Weibel, S. (1996b). Prologue is Past. September 27. Available E-mail: IMAGE-METADATA-CONF-L@oclc.org.

Weibel, S. (1996c). A proposed convention for embedding metadata in HTML. Available: http://www.oclc.org:5046/~weibel/html-meta.html.

Weibel, S. (1996d). RE:Core—current status. December 19. Available E-mail: IMAGE-METADATA-CONF-L@oclc.org.

Weibel, S., Godby, J., Miller, E., and Daniel, R. (1995). OCLC/NCSA metadata workshop report. Available: http://purl.oclc.org/metadata/dublin_core_report.html.

Xu, A. (1996). Accessing information on the Internet: Feasibility study of USMARC format and AACR2. Available: http://www.oclc.org/oclc/man/colloq/xu.htm.

Young, A. P., and Peters, T. A. (1996). Reinventing Alexandria: Managing change in the electronic library. *Journal of Library Administration* **22**(2/3), 21–41.

Preservation and Collection Development in Academic Libraries of the United States

Joint History and Future Prospects: A Review Article

Sara R. Williams
University Libraries
University of Colorado at Boulder
Boulder, Colorado 80309

Diane Lunde
Colorado State University Libraries
Fort Collins, Colorado 80523

I. Introduction

Librarians have always performed two basic functions: they have chosen books for their collections and sought to protect those collections from damage, loss, and deterioration. Although "book selection" and "repair" of library materials have long been addressed in the library literature, "collection development" and "preservation" as professional specialties within librarianship are developments of the latter part of the 20th century. Both specialties developed in the late 1960s and early 1970s in response to changes in the demands made by American higher education on libraries and their collections. The two fields became specialties at about the same time and underwent periods of uncertainty about their organizational structure and the scope of their authority.

By the 1980s, collection development was a well articulated discipline, with a core body of literature as characterized by general bibliographies, several prominent authorities, and an extensive body of research. Several periodicals were introduced to address the special concerns of the discipline (*Collection Management*, *Collection Building*, and the related *Library Acquisitions: Practice and Theory*) with widespread discussion of collection development topics in related library journals, including *Technical Services Quarterly* and

0065-2830/97 $25.00

Library Resources and Technical Services. Numerous textbooks were written for the instruction of new students of the field (Curley and Broderick, 1985; Katz, 1980; Broadus, 1981; Gardner, 1981; Magrill and Corbin, 1989; Wortman, 1989; Osborn and Atkinson, 1991; Evans, 1987).

In contrast, the literature of preservation, while certainly not scarce, developed more slowly. Although some may argue that preservation has not yet developed an equivalent intellectual and theoretical structure, standard preservation works have been published (Cunha and Cunha, 1971–1972, 1983; Morrow and Walker, 1983; DePew, 1991; and Swartzburg, 1995) with a core body of knowledge being identified (Fox, 1988). Specialized periodicals for preservation appeared at about the same time as collection development, including *Conservation Administration News* (*CAN*), *Abbey Newsletter* and its sister publication *Alkaline Paper Advocate*, and *Restaurator*. The fact that preservation has from its beginnings been regarded more of a technical field has been reflected in the publication of many strongly practical "how to" manuals in conservation treatment procedures (Horton, 1969; Greenfield, 1983; Kyle, 1983; Morrow and Dyal, 1986).

Although both fields would appear to have plenty of basic issues in common, as they are both concerned with library collection materials, each has chosen to address the issues differently. Not until the late 1980s and early 1990s has there been much discussion on interdisciplinary issues. The application of electronic technologies and development of electronic resources in libraries has fostered the commonality of concerns about the "preservation" or "archiving" of information and the access to information.

The purpose of this chapter is to review the literature to describe the fields of collection development and preservation as they have evolved and functioned in the past, the evolving interrelationships of the two fields, and the challenges in the future that may bring them toward a closer interrelationship of theory and practice.

II. Origins and Growth of Collection Development

"Collection development," as the professional term used to define the systematic selection and building of library collections, was not used until the second half of the twentieth century. While the discussion of selection for public libraries produced a vigorous growth of literature from about 1870, academic libraries, with rare exceptions, left selection responsibilities to the parent institution's faculty. It was not unusual for the actual book budget to be under faculty, rather than library, control. The librarian's role was seen as one of acquisition, management, and maintenance, not selection.

Although librarians occasionally criticized this division of responsibility as unsystematic, there appeared to be no real incentive to change these traditional arrangements (Broadus, 1991, pp.8–9). During and immediately after World War II, fundamental changes began to occur in American higher education that affected both teaching methods and the rationale behind library selection. Area studies programs developed, partly in response to the need for information on foreign countries and cultures to support the defense effort (Hay, 1990, p.12). After the war, large numbers of discharged servicemen sought to continue their education by means of federal aid. Geiger (1993, p.251) reports that enough of these "GI Bill" students continued into graduate school to effectively double the number of Ph.Ds produced from 1940 to 1950.

When the launching of Sputnik in 1958 triggered a decades-long era of United States–Soviet competition, the United States government invested enormous sums in efforts to increase the nation's capacity for scientific research. The large sums available for research gave it a greater value to universities and increased the power and prestige of graduate education. Academic teaching at this time shifted from the lecture-textbook method to a greater emphasis on seminars and research problems. Efforts were made to draw students into active research at an earlier stage of their academic life (Magrill and East, 1978, p.11). Specialization within disciplines increased, with more faculty publishing at a greater rate in increasingly specialized subject areas (Gerdeman Thompson, 1984, pp.34–35). Faculty demanded more comprehensive collections to support research while, at the same time, the rapid proliferation of published material made leisurely selection by faculty committees impractical (Magrill and East, 1978, p.6).

It was during this period that academic libraries began to lay claim to selection responsibilities. The shift in responsibility was gradual but steady, and by the 1980s selection by librarians was more nearly the rule than the exception in academic libraries. In an early study, Byrd reported that between 1963 and 1966 Indiana University Library established 10 subject specialist positions, whose primary responsibilities were book selection, advanced reference service, and faculty liaison. The positions were justified on the grounds that interdisciplinary programs in social sciences, humanities, and area studies departments could not longer be adequately served by general reference librarians (Byrd, 1966, pp.191–192). By 1978, Wilmer H. Baatz, in his survey of collection development in ARL libraries, expressed surprise at the amount of selection done by librarians rather than faculty (Baatz, 1978, p.100). The withdrawal of faculty participation in the 19 libraries he studied appeared to be greater than many librarians wished: "Many librarians lamented to me that it was difficult to get significant faculty assistance and advice, that either the interest was not there . . . or that the faculty felt the selection was being carried out at least adequately and believed the librarian should carry out the duties!" (Baatz, 1978, p.97).

It was assumed from the beginning that, if subject bibliographers were to perform what had hitherto been a faculty function, they must have subject expertise similar to that of faculty. Early descriptions of the subject bibliographers role made it clear that this was to be a specialty in which subject knowledge was to be at least as important as knowledge of librarianship, if not more so. Margit Kraft, in a paper criticizing the ballooning size of most American research collections, called for rigorously educated subject specialists to take over book selection, on the grounds that such full-time librarian scholars could make more disciplined selection decisions. These were to be full-time scholars, trained in ". . . the history of ideas, the history of science, epistemology, and the necessary bibliographic tools" (1967, p.295). Haro, in another early paper, described the ideal bibliographer as ". . . an advanced reference librarian, a researcher, an instructor in library use, a vital communication link between the library and appropriate academic departments, and a friend to the students" (1969, p.164). The bibliographer must have an extensive scholarly background in his subject, including an advanced degree and ". . . proficiency in one or more foreign languages," for faculty would only agree to relinquish their selection responsibilities to a bibliographer with credentials similar to their own (Haro, 1969, p.166). Such high conceptions of the bibliographer's scholarly role were not universally accepted. Helen Welch Tuttle (1969, p.170) immediately pointed out that the kind of bibliographic specialist Haro described would need to be "at least quintuplets" to do the job. Some questions were also raised as to whether libraries could offer sufficient incentives to attract and retain scholars with such extensive credentials. The depressed market for academic teaching jobs in the 1970s created a pool of displaced Ph.Ds who were willing to consider library careers (Haskell, 1984, p.79), but this source of potential bibliographers began to dry up within 10 years. A serious question also existed as to whether librarians would necessarily accept scholars as colleagues, no matter how impressive their qualifications, if they lacked credentials in library science. Less than a decade after Haro and Tuttle's exchange of views on the topic, Ann Coppin had redefined the optimal qualifications for a subject specialist as undergraduate and master's degrees in the disciplinary subject, plus an MLS. While Coppin found the prospect of a subject doctorate in addition to the MLS "pleasant to contemplate," she was skeptical about the ability of libraries to offer adequate incentives to attract Ph.Ds into the field: "The degree in librarianship is required because many librarians are not ready to accept as librarian anyone who does not have this degree" (1974, p.126). A few years later Elizabeth Futas dismissed the subject Ph.D as nonessential: "Why get a second-rate historian when you could get a first-rate librarian? (1982, p.56).

As the shift to selection by librarians got underway, decisions had to be made on how to organize and staff this relatively new function. Most libraries had an acquisitions office of some kind, but it soon became apparent that "collection development" would include more than order, receipt, and payment responsibilities. The organizational issue was further complicated by the fact that collection development functions did not fit neatly into the technical services–public services division around which most major research libraries were organized. Baatz (1978, p.113) reported a certain amount of friction between bibliographers and technical services staff, usually over the prioritization of jobs and turnaround time. He also noted that bibliographers were often viewed as elitists in their own organizations; bibliographers, in turn, complained of lack of institutional support and recognition (Baatz, 1978, p.117). When Jeanne Sohn did her survey of ARL libraries in 1987, no single organizational pattern had emerged as dominant: "Apparently each library has determined an organizational pattern that fit its own overall structure given the restrictions of budget, personnel, politics, or innumerable other factors" (p.131).

Ironically, it was the very abundance of both money and potential new materials during this early period that forced libraries into changes that made collection development less of an intellectual specialty and more of a managerial specialty for which scholarly credentials were unnecessary. The sixties and early seventies were characterized by large materials budgets and rapid expansion of research collections. This era has acquired a nostalgic glow in the minds of many librarians, although the literature of the period indicates that the bountiful budgets were accompanied by a certain amount of stress and anxiety. Librarians sought systematic methods of managing existing collections and the vast amount of new scholarly material that was suddenly available; the kind of intellectually rigorous, research-based selection envisaged by Kraft and Haro turned out to be feasible only in rare cases. As early as 1978 Baatz reported that 12 of the 18 libraries he studied had approval plans for U.S. imprints. Approval plans were viewed as providing a means to make up for lack of subject specialists, to save on staff expenses, and to ensure prompt receipt of needed materials. The idea of delegating even partial selection authority to a vendor, however, did not meet with universal approval: "Several collection development librarians expressed concern that the quality of the collection could suffer over the next 20–30 years with the majority of the selection being done by dealer employees . . . as compared to the selection being done by librarians on site who know the curricula and the research needs of their primary clientele" (Baatz, 1978, pp.94–95).

This increasing acceptance of approval plans as a selection tool marks the beginning of a reorientation of collection development's view of itself and of the role of the subject bibliographer, from an intellectual discipline to a managerial role. As materials funding became more constricted during the 1980s, the disciplinary literature began to refer as frequently to "collection management" as to "collection development" (Futas, 1995, pp.3–4), with "collection management" defined as ". . . the systemic, efficient and economic stewardship of library resources" (Mosher, 1982, p.45). Just as the term "collection development" marked a shift in professional emphasis from the individual title to the the collection as an entity in itself, so "collection management" represented an expansion of collection development to encompass all activities in cultivation and care of the collection. As demands on library budgets increased, greater attention had to be focused on effective management of existing collections, involving bibliographers to a greater extent with such formerly marginal activities as collection evaluation, maintenance, weeding, storage, and preservation. "Reselection" of existing collections could be as time consuming, if not more so, than the selection of new materials, resulting in a total management to better serve the needs of current and future scholarship (Cogswell, 1987, p.270). Many library articles during this time were devoted to collection evaluation, collection surveys, use studies, and citation analysis, all measuring the effective match of selection choices against library patron needs. The bibliographer over time became less the research scholar envisaged by Kraft and Haro and more of a manager of increasingly scarce resources. Marcia Pankake, writing in 1984, tried to relate contemporary concerns in collection development to historical trends in American librarianship, but also conceded that "Major concerns in collection development today are neither title-oriented (bibliographic) nor explicitly value-oriented factors, although both still exist. Newer concerns are instead process oriented" (p.206).

By the 1990s, emphasis had shifted from collection building by careful selection of significant titles to the management of access to sources of information, which might or might not be owned by the library itself. Continuing financial pressures plus a plethora of new media tended to increase the focus on process and on getting as much as possible from the contemporary publishing output, whether in conventional or electronic form. Karen A. Schmidt organized her bibliographic essay on the collection development literature for 1989 around such topics as "finance," "serials," and "new technology" and gave it the rather "indicative" title "Lives of Noisy Desperation" (Schmidt, 1990).

III. Origins and Growth of Preservation

The beginning of preservation as a discipline within librarianship is popularly assumed to be the Florence flood of November, 1966 and the international recovery operation which followed it (Allison, 1992, p.517). But librarians and bookbinders had been discussing preservation questions for at least a century before the Arno overflowed its banks. In 1901, Douglas Cockerell, in his *Bookbinding and the Care of Books*, decried the poor quality of contemporary papers and bookbinding leathers and devoted a chapter to the "injurious influences" which caused books to deteriorate (pp.291–301). McDonald has documented evidence that preservation of their collections was a source of professional concern to librarians as early as 1876, when the newly formed American Library Association's first annual conference included a session on book deterioration (McDonald, 1990, pp.484–485). Concern was expressed early on about the quality of materials. In Britain, the Royal Society of Arts created a Committee on the Deterioration of Paper in 1897, and the U.S. Leather and Paper Laboratory, created by the Bureau of Chemistry of the Department of Agriculture, conducted extensive research on the causes of paper deterioration in the first decade of the twentieth century (Higgenbotham, 1990a, pp.501, 506). Higgenbotham's treatise *Our Past Preserved* (1990b) presents a detailed history of American library preservation during those early years.

Much of the discussion over the past century focused on environmental factors such as building design and on agitation for some kind of standards for binding (Higgenbotham, 1990a, pp.496–497). The emphasis on binding and storage conditions is significant; preservation was defined at an early state in its development as a managerial or technical function, a definition which has persisted in part to the present day. When *Library Resources and Technical Services* began publishing its series of "Year's Work" bibliographic essays, the few preservation titles which appeared were discussed under the heading "binding and conservation of materials" (Tauber, 1964, pp.109–110). The works cited in Tauber's essay on the literature for 1963 were W.J. Barrow's *Permanence/Durability of the Book*, the Library Binding Institute's *Library Binding Handbook* (1963), and *Protecting the Library and Its Resources: A Guide to Physical Protection and Insurance* by the ALA Library Technology Project (1963). Most of the articles discussed in later essays were on similar topics. Preservation titles continued to be discussed under the rubric of technical services until 1980, when Rose Mary Magrill linked preservation with collection development, although there is little crossover in her discussion of the topics. Beginning in 1981 preservation was given its own annual review article reflecting both the stature that the field had attained and the increasing volume of publications on the topic.

While the Florence flood of 1966 may not be the beginning of preservation as a field, it did trigger an escalation of interest in the subject of book and paper deterioration. As early as 1967 the Library of Congress developed a pilot project to compare the degree of embrittlement of its collections with those of other libraries and to test the feasibility of identifying a "national preservation collection," which could be stored in stable environmental conditions, perhaps in a cave or mineshaft (Shaffer, 1969, p.11). The formation of the Committee on Preservation of Library Materials in 1970 further enhanced the professionalism of preservation. Ten years later the committee achieved full section status in the American Library Association, becoming the Preservation of Library Materials Section (PLMS).

Although many academic libraries housed basic repair and commercial binding activities, in the early 1970s they came to acknowledge that preservation was a necessary function, although, as Walker remarks, it was ". . . often assigned a low priority due to insufficient funds or personnel and the lack of large-scale technical solutions." When Walker (1975, pp.39–40) surveyed 115 academic libraries with holdings of 500,000 volumes or more, 62 of the 86 institutions responding carried on some kind of preservation activity, although often at a minimal level.

As if to counteract widespread ignorance, apathy, or hopelessness with regard to the deterioration of the nation's collections, much of the literature from this period rings with an almost evangelistic fervor. Those committed to preservation felt an urgency to convince librarians, funding agencies, and the public of the existence of the problem. The film *Slow Fires: On Preservation of the Human Record* (1987) provided both a vivid image for the deterioration of acidic paper and an emotional plea for urgent action. There were also numerous articles of the "how to" variety, giving specific instruction to librarians on why and how to take measures to protect their collections. The series of articles published in *Library Journal* in 1979 is a good example of the tone of much of the early literature (Banks, 1979; Berger, 1979; Bohem, 1979; Darling, 1979a,b; Harris, 1979; Koda, 1979, Patterson, 1979), in that the authors attempted to provide some practical information for use at the local level, as well as to draw attention to the scope of the national problem. The tone of these and many similar articles alternated a strong sense of alarm with a more optimistic belief that, given prompt and vigorous action at all levels, the catastrophe could be averted.

Since the United States does not have a national library as such, the nation's research collections are scattered among multiple institutions across the country. Several of these libraries had designed programs to address the needs of their own collections, but it was clear that a broader, more collaborative strategy would be necessary to address the problem effectively (Battin, 1992, p.42). It was also clear that no single institution could or would fund such a massive campaign and that federal funding would be essential. John H. Hammer has described the highly successful campaign orchestrated by the Council on Library Resources, the Commission on Preservation and Access, the National Endowment for the Humanities, and other groups (Hammer, 1992). It was made clear, however, from the beginning that federal support was conditional on the promise that the proposed national preservation initiative would improve public access to research materials as well as preserve them (Hammer, 1992, p.35).

The national preservation effort had from the beginning, therefore, three basic assumptions: (1) given that research collections were assumed to be in imminent danger of deterioration, any solution must be comprehensive enough to save a reasonably representative sample of those collections in a comparatively short period of time; (2) the program must be efficient in terms of both productivity and cost per unit; and (3) to meet expectations of improved access, the end product must be distributable to other libraries at reasonable cost. Patricia Battin describes the process by which the Commission on Preservation and Access developed a strategy which, while "admittedly incomplete," had the potential to save the most books in the least time at the least cost (i.e., a massive microfilming effort aimed at the one-third of the nation's research collections presumed to be in the most danger). Filming was to be nonduplicative and carried out to exacting standards, with access provided via a national bibliographic utility (Battin, 1992, p.44). This strategy formed the basis for a series of large, grant-funded, subject-based microfilming projects, which have been so successful as to all but define the field of preservation. Child (1992), Farr (1992), and McClung (1992) in their studies have described the history and development of these projects. It will be enough here to say that the cooperative microfilming projects of the late 1980s and early 1990s were immensely successful. The philosophy which lay behind them, however, was vigorously criticized almost as soon as the projects began.

The selection criteria for cooperative microfilming projects eventually evolved by the Research Libraries Group were developed by a task force including both preservationists and collection development officers and were traditional in that they were based on specific subject collections developed by the participating institutions. The assumption was that the so-called "great collections" (i.e., large subject collections accumulated by recognized research libraries), were probably worth preserving without further discussion (Child, 1992, pp.150–151). The definition of a "great collection" was never seriously in question; the landmark articles by Atkinson (1986) and Child (1986) provided comprehensive discussions that have never been superseded.

But the massive microfilming projects, while achieving the goals initially set for them, left a number of serious issues unaddressed and shaped the nature and practice of preservation in ways that not everyone found desirable. By the criteria which defined them major reformatting projects inevitably concentrated on material which was not in high current demand. External funding was therefore available for books that were seldom called for, while the task of keeping high-demand titles in usable condition was supposed to be absorbed by the institution's own operating budget. Barclay W. Ogden (1987) called a fundamental assumption of mass reformatting into question in a paper which demonstrated that materials which were merely brittle, but not heavily used, were in less immediate danger than had been thought. Hazen (1990) took issue with the presumed need for haste, the commitment to microfilm which made preservation equivalent to reformatting, and the apparent abandonment of local collections and needs. In Hazen's view, the alignment of preservation with mass reformatting effectively separated it from its own origins: "This model passes over the equally prominent, longer lived preservationist stream that focuses on library materials as physical objects that people actually use, and on local library collections as distinct and meaningful entities in support of scholarship" (Hazen, 1990, p.346). By the early 1990s, preservation had effectively divided into two tracks: cooperative projects devoted to mass reformatting of subject-based collections and funded by private or federal grants and locally organized and funded initiatives focused on the traditional preservation operations of binding, repair, and conservation. Maralyn Jones, in her bibliographic essay on the disciplinary literature for 1990, noted uneasily that the field of preservation appeared to suffer from a serious lack of consensus on goals and priorities: "Part of the field . . . manages programs that, slowly and at great expense, maintain physical collections . . . that support current faculty scholarship and curricula. The other, unrelated, part oversees the replacement of hundreds of thousands of about-to-disappear brittle volumes that are rarely consulted except by devotees of the arcane and antique" (Jones, 1991, p.294). And yet the two tracks, one devoted to reformatting of information and the other which continues to carry out traditional operations to maintain objects, have one goal: the preservation of scholarship for the present and future use by whatever means and regardless of physical format. In acknowledgment of this essential unity of purpose, the Preservation of Library Materials Section (PLMS) and the Reproduction of Library Materials Section (RLMS), the two groups within the Association for Library Collections and Technical Services (ALCTS) devoted to the preservation and reformatting issues, merged to form the Preservation and Reformatting Section (PARS).

IV. Interdisciplinary Nature of Collection Development and Preservation

Collection development and preservation have evolved into mutually reinforcing disciplines centered on collections as whole entities. Collection development has traditionally centered its attention on the intellectual processes of selection; preservation has developed the more technical focus on maintaining collection usability. Together the two fields manage collections "from the cradle to the grave"; the cradle being the selection of materials and the grave the ultimate decision to discard.

Until the 1970s and 1980s, however, there was not much discussion of the interdisciplinary nature of both fields. As mentioned previously, most preservation literature was of the practical nature, discussing the technical aspects of collection maintenance, repair, binding, and environmental controls. If collection development texts mentioned preservation, it was related to collection maintenance activities such as weeding and storage. Curley felt that this type of discussion followed naturally "because one of the reasons for weeding a collection is to identify the materials that are in poor physical condition" (Curley and Broderick, 1985, p. 313). Materials thus identified could be preserved, replaced, sent to storage, or withdrawn. But as increased professional attention was paid to collection management and as preservation became a full-fledged speciality within librarianship, collection development texts added detailed discussion on preservation issues. In his treatise, Wortman (1989, pp.179–210) presents a very balanced chapter on preservation program elements.

During the 1980s, the increasing need to find a solution to the problem of brittle books began to bring collection development and preservation into a closer working interrelationship. The change in emphasis in collection development to collection management of entire collections and the development of preservation as a professional speciality field has already been discussed. Constructive work was done by professionals in both fields on such issues as selection for preservation, cooperative and resource sharing at the state and regional levels, and the emergence of new formats for the creation, delivery, and access to information. The questions of access vs ownership clearly has implications for both disciplines. This period saw the creation of the Commission on Preservation and Access, several state and regional preservation cooperative organizations, and the ARL/OMS preservation studies program.

An intellectual structure for choosing materials for reformatting and conservation treatment was necessary to successfully address the problem of embrittlement. "Selection for preservation" became the expression of choice to describe the theory and policy of identifying and selecting those materials that were physically in an endangered physical condition and warranted preservation. Many of the early works were written by collection development librarians and presented the intellectual framework for making preservation selection decisions. Rutstein (1982, p.325) stated that the same "informational and disposal criteria" should be employed during selection/accession process, maintenance (including preservation), and collection surveys and inventories.

Hazen noted that "preservation specialists are best suited to identify the endangered materials within a particular collection, but subject specialists must then delineate priorities among those items" (1982, p.8). Holland (1984) looked at various selection strategies from a preservationist point of view. In his landmark article on selection for preservation, Atkinson described a typology of three classes of materials, ranking them in order of priority and institutional responsibility for preservation. He also advocated a coordinated program for "Class 3 Preservation," the less-used research materials of regional or national importance (Atkinson, 1986). In her response to Atkinson in the same issue, Child (1986) gave possible mechanisms for actually identifying collections for Class 3 preservation microfilming. Numerous authors have expanded on the topic in the past 10 years including Brown and Gertz (1989), Child (1992), Bansa (1992), and Riecken (1992). The overriding viewpoint has been that the intellectual value of the item as defined by collection development determines the preservation predence.

Also in the 1980s the Association of Research Libraries Office of Management Services began its sponsored self-study program to enable academic libraries to identify and address librarywide preservation problems. Along with a study of library resources, organizational issues, library environment and disaster control issues, each library undertook a study of the physical condition of its collection. Thc sclf-study helped raise awareness of preservation needs at the local level and provided a plan for future development of a preservation program to address the discovered problems (Darling *el al.*, 1987). The fact that the participation in the study process involved staff from across the library organization helped the staff to discover the inherent interrelationship of all library activities, particularly preservation and collection management.

New information technologies provide another common concern, as electronic technology can be used both as a preservation technology for saving deteriorating collections and to provide additional access to new information sources. They also provide a challenge to preservation and collection development in developing joint policies and procedures to preserve the new ever-evolving formats and to archive the new information so that it too will be available for the foreseeable future. Shoaf (1996, p. 238) addresses these issues in his article on preservation and digitization noting that access issues and preservation needs will become further linked in the library of the twenty-first century.

V. Conclusion

Both preservation and collection development owe their development as professional specialties to an extraordinary combination of circumstances in the history of American higher education. The expansion of the teaching and research roles of American universities in the post-war and post-Sputnik decades forced a change in the traditional role of the teaching faculty in the building of library collections and offered librarians the possibility of a new, more intellectual function. Preservation was given its impetus from a set of emergency circumstances: a literal flood and a metaphorical fire. A well-planned political campaign in both the public arena and within the profession gave preservation legitimacy, but at the price of the perception that it was essentially an emergency function to be funded as much as possible from outside the institution.

As the century draws to a close, the original impetus which funded the expansion of library collections and the drive to preserve them has begun to fade. Cultural institutions, including libraries, can no longer expect to be regarded as unquestioned public goods. The increasing cost of higher education is no longer being borne without a murmur by students and taxpayers. Library administrators now talk more frequently of access than of ownership, on the assumption that some collection other than their own will have to meet a significant portion of their users' needs. Preservation programs which have grown and matured on a steady diet of federal funding can no longer assume that the nation's bounty will continue unchecked. Libraries must compete now for commitment from their institutions, as well as for dollars.

Shrinking funds and the proliferation of new information media will inevitably force collection development professionals further into the position of managing access to the current literature, in whatever form that literature may take. While electronic media offer wonderful opportunities for new and creative ways to present information, the belief that soon all relevant information will be available in electronic form is probably visionary. The idea that the entire historical research collection of this, or any, country will someday be painlessly made available via the World Wide Web or its successors ignores the substantial cost of building a retrospective electronic collection. Research libraries will, by default, be dealing with mixed collections consisting of new, electronic publications and a large historical paper collection for many years to come. The management of this retrospective mixed collection is the responsibility of both preservation and collection development, who must intermesh their expertise in the building an intellectual structure for decision making and in developing managerial and conservation skills that are necessary to deal coherently and creatively with the continuing challenge of building our collections and maintaining access to those collections.

References

ALA Library Technology Project (1963). *Protecting the Library and Its Resources: A Guide to Physical Protection and Insurance.* American Library Association, Chicago.

Allison, T. L. (1992). Toward a shared enterprise: Western European and U.S. preservation programs. *Collection Management* **15,** 517–525.

Atkinson, R. W. (1986). Selection for preservation: A materialistic approach. *Library Resources and Technical Services* **30,** 341–353.

Baatz, W. H. (1978). Collection development in 19 libraries of the Association of Research Libraries. *Library Acquisitions: Practice and Theory* **2,** 85–121.

Banks, P. N. (1979). Education for conservators. *Library Journal* **104,** 1013–1017.

Bansa, H. (1992). Selection for conservation. *Restaurator* **13,** 193–197.

Barrow, W. J. (1963). *Permanence/Durability of the Book.* W. J. Barrow Research Laboratory, Richmond, VA.

Battin, P. (1992). "As far into the future as possible': Choice and cooperation in the 1990s. In *Advances in Preservation and Access* (B. B. Higgenbotham and M. E. Jackson, ed.), Vol. 1, pp. 41–48. Meckler, Westport, CT.

Berger, P. (1979). Minor repairs in a small research library. *Library Journal* **104,** 1311–1317.

Bohem, H. (1979). Regional conservation services. *Library Journal* **104,** 1428–1431.

Broadus, R. N. (1981). *Selecting Materials for Libraries,* 2nd ed. Wilson, New York.

Broadus, R. N. (1991). The history of collection development. In *Collection Management: A New Treatise* (C. B. Osborn and R. Atkinson, eds.), Foundations in Library and Information Science, Vol. 26A), pp. 3–28. JAI Press, Greenwich, CT.

Brown, C. B., and Gertz, J. E. (1989) 'Selection for preservation': Applications for college libraries. In *Building on the First Century: Proceedings of the Fifth National Conference of the Association of College and Research Libraries, Cincinnati, Ohio, April 5–8, 1989* (J. C. Fennell, ed.), pp. 288–294. Association of College and Research Libraries, Chicago.

Byrd, C. K. (1966). Subject specialists in a university library. *College & Research Libraries* **27,** 191–193.

Child, M. S. (1986). Further thoughts on Selection for preservation: A materialistic approach'. *Library Resources and Technical Services* **30,** 354–362.

Child, M. S. (1992). Selection for preservation. In *Advances in Preservation and Access* (B. B. Higgenbotham and M. E. Jackson, eds.), Vol. 1, pp. 147–158. Meckler, Westport, CT.

Cockerell, D. (1991). *Bookbinding and the Care of Books: A Handbook for Amateurs, Bookbinders and Librarians.* Lyons & Burford, New York. Originally published: Appleton, New York, 1901.

Cogswell, J. A. (1987). The organization of collection management functions in academic research libraries. *Journal of Academic Librarianship* **13,** 268–276.

Coppin, A. (1974) The subject specialist on the academic library staff. *Libri* **24,** 122–128.

Cunha, G. M., and Cunha, D. G. (1971–1972). *Conservation of Library Materials: A Manual and Bibliography on the Care, Repair, and Restoration of Library Materials,* 2nd ed. Scarecrow Press, Metuchen, N.J.

Cunha, G. M., and Cunha, D. G. (1983). *Library and Archives Conservation: 1980s and Beyond.* Scarecrow Press, Metuchen, N.J.

Curley, A., and Broderick, D. (1985). *Building Library Collections,* 6th ed. Scarecrow Press, Metuchen, NJ.

Darling, P. W. (1979a). Towards a nationwide preservation program. *Library Journal* **104,** 1012.

Darling, P. W. (1979b). Preservation epilogue: Signs of hope. *Library Journal* **104,** 1627.

Darling, P. W., with Webster, D. E., Harris, C., and Merrill-Oldham, J. (1987). *Preservation Planning Program: An Assisted Self-Study Manual for Libraries,* Expanded 1987 ed. Association of Research Libraries, Office of Management Studies, Washington, DC.

DePew, J. N. (1991). *A Library, Media, and Archival Preservation Handbook.* ABC- CLIO, Santa Barbara, CA.

Evans, G. E. (1987). *Developing Library and Information Center Collections,* 2nd ed., Library Science Text Series. Libraries Unlimited, Littleton, CO.

Farr, G. F., Jr. (1992). NEH's program for the preservation of brittle books. In *Advances in Preservation and Access* (B. B. Higgenbotham and M. E. Jackson, eds.), Vol. 1, pp. 49–60. Meckler, Westport, CT.

Fox, L. L., comp. (1988). *A Core Collection in Preservation.* Resources and Technical Services Division, American Library Association, Chicago.

Futas, E. (1982). Issues in collection development: Wanted: Collection development officer. *Collection Building* **4,** 55–56.

Futas, E., ed. (1995). *Collection Development Policies and Procedures,* 3rd ed. Oryx Press, Phoenix, AZ.

Gardner, R. K. (1981). *Library Collections: Their Origin, Selection, and Development.* McGraw-Hill, New York.

Geiger, R. (1993). Research, graduate education, and the ecology of American universities: An interpretive history." In *The European and American University since 1800: Historical and Sociological Essays* (S. Rothblatt and B. Wittrock, eds.), pp. 234–259. Cambridge University Press, New York.

Gerdeman Thompson, J. (1984). *The Modern Idea of the University* (American University Studies, Series 14: Education, Vol. 2). Peter Lang, New York.

Greenfield, J. (1983). *Books: Their Care and Repair.* Wilson, New York.

Hammer, J. H. (1992). On the political aspects of book preservation in the U.S. In *Advances in Preservation and Access* (B. B. Higgenbotham and M. E. Jackson, eds.), Vol. 1, pp. 22–40. Meckler, Westport, CT.

Haro, R. P. (1969). The bibliographer in the academic library. *Library Resources and Technical Services* **13,** 163–169.

Harris, C. (1979). Mass deacidification. *Library Journal* **104,** 1423–1427.

Haskell, J. D., Jr. (1984). Subject bibliographers in academic libraries: An historical and descriptive review. In *Advances in Library Administration and Organization* (G. B. McCabe and B. Kreissman, eds.), Vol. 3, pp. 73–84. JAI Press, Greenwich, CT.

Hay, F. J. (1990). The subject specialist in the academic library: A review article. *Journal of Academic Librarianship* **16,** 11–17.

Hazen, D. C. (1982). Collection development, collection management, and preservation. *Library Resources and Technical Services* **26,** 3–11.

Hazen, D. C. (1990). Preservation in poverty and plenty: Policy issues for the 1990s. *Journal of Academic Librarianship* **15,** 344–351.

Higgenbotham, B. B. (1990a). The Brittle books problem: A turn-of-the-century perspective. *Libraries & Culture* **25,** 496–512.

Higgenbotham, B. B. (1990b). *Our Past Preserved: A History of American Library Preservation, 1876-1910.* G. K. Hall, Boston.

Holland, M. E. (1984). Material selection for library conservation. *Library & Archival Security* **6,** 7–21.

Horton, C. (1969). *Cleaning and Preserving Bindings and Related Materials,* 2nd rev. ed., LTP Publ. No. 16. Library Technology Program, American Library Association, Chicago.

Jones, M. (1991). More than ten years after: identity and direction in library preservation. *Library Resources and Technical Services* **35,** 294–306.

Katz, W. A. (1980). *Collection Development: The Selection of Materials for Libraries.* Holt, Rinehart & Winston, New York.

Koda, P. S. (1979). The Analytical bibliographer and the conservator. *Library Journal* **104,** 1623–1626.

Kraft, M. (1967). An argument for selectivity in the acquisition of materials for research libraries. *Library Quarterly* **37,** 284–395.

Kyle, H. (1983). *Library Materials Preservation Manual: Practical Methods for Preserving Books, Pamphlets and Other Printed Materials.* Nicholas T. Smith, Bronxville, NY.

Library Binding Institute (1963). *Library Binding Handbook.* Library Binding Institute, Boston.

Magrill, R. M. (1980). Collection development and preservation in 1979. *Library Resources and Technical Services* **24,** 247–273.

Magrill, R. M., and Corbin, J. (1989). *Acquisitions Management and Collection Development in Libraries,* 2nd ed. American Library Association, Chicago.

Magrill, R. M., and East, M. (1978). Collection development in large university libraries. In *Advances in Librarianship* (M. H. Harris, ed.), Vol. 8, pp. 1–54. Academic Press, New York.

McClung, P. A. (1992). Consortial action: RLG's preservation program. In *Advances in Preservation and Access* (B. B. Higgenbotham and M. E. Jackson, eds.), Vol. 1, pp. 61–70. Meckler, Westport, CT.

McDonald, L. (1990). Forgotten forebears: Concerns with preservation, 1876 to World War I. *Libraries & Culture* **25,** 483–495.

Morrow, C. C., and Dyal, C. (1986). *Conservation Treatment Procedures: A Manual of Step-by-Step Procedures for the Maintenance and Repair of Library Materials,* 2nd ed. Libraries Unlimited, Littleton, CO.

Morrow, C. C., with Walker, G. (1983). *The Preservation Challenge: A Guide to Conserving Library Materials.* Knowledge Industry Publications, White Plains, NY.

Mosher, P. H. (1982). Collection development to collection management: Toward stewardship of library resources. *Collection Management* **4,** 41–48.

Ogden, B. W. (1987). Preservation selection and treatment options. In *Preservation: A Research Library Priority. Minutes of the 111th Meeting of the Association of Research Libraries,* pp. 38–42. Association of Research Libraries, Washington, DC.

Osborn, C. B., and Atkinson, R., eds. (1991). *Collection Management: A New Treatise* (Foundations in Library and Information Science, Vol. 26A and Vol. 26B). JAI Press, Greenwich, CT.

Pankake, M. (1984). From book selection to collection management: Continuity and advance in an unending work. In *Advances in Librarianship* (W. Simonton, ed.), Vol. 13, pp. 185–210. Academic Press, New York.

Patterson, R. H. (1979). Organizing for conservation. *Library Journal* **104,** 1116–1119.

Riecken, H. (1992). Selection for preservation of research library materials. *ACLS Newsletter* **2,** 10–12.

Rutstein, J. S. (1982). Preservation and collection development: Establishing the connection. In *Options for the 80s: Proceedings of the Second National Conference of the Association of College and Research Libraries* (M. D. Kathman and V. F. Massman, eds.), Foundations in Library and Information Science, Vol. 17, pp. 321–329. JAI Press, Greenwich, CT.

Schmidt, K. A. (1990). Lives of noisy desperation: A year's work in collection development, 1989. *Library Resources and Technical Services* **34,** 433–443.

Shaffer, N. J. (1969). The Library of Congress pilot preservation project. *College & Research Libraries* **30,** 5–11.

Shoaf, E. C. (1996). Preservation and digitization: Trends and implications. In *Advances in Librarianship* (I. Godden, ed.), Vol. 20, pp. 223–239. Academic Press, San Diego, CA.

Slow Fires: On the Preservation of the Human Record (1987). Sponsored by Council on Library Resources, the National Endowment for the Humanities, and the Andrew W. Mellon Foundation. American Film Foundation, Santa Monica, CA.

Sohn, J. (1987). Collection development organizational patterns in ARL libraries. *Library Resources and Technical Services* **31,** 123–134.

Swartzburg, S. G. (1995). *Preserving Library Materials: A Manual,* 2nd ed. Scarecrow Press, Metuchen, NJ.

Tauber, M. F. (1964). Technical services in 1963. *Library Resources and Technical Services* **8,** 101–111.

Tuttle, H. W. (1969). An acquisitionist looks at Mr. Haro's bibliographer. *Library Resources and Technical Services* **13,** 170–174.

Walker, G. (1975). Preservation efforts in larger U.S. academic libraries. *College & Research Libraries* **36,** 39–44.

Wortman, W. A. (1989). *Collection Management: Background and Principles.* American Library Association, Chicago.

Values in College and University Library Mission Statements

A Search for Distinctive Beliefs, Meaning, and Organizational Culture

Stephanie Rogers Bangert
Saint Mary's College of California
Saint Albert Hall Library
Moraga, California 94575

I. Introduction

Higher education in the United States is increasingly under scrutiny. The tax-paying public, legislators, and students themselves are all watching colleges and universities with a critical eye. Inflation, reduced federal support, a declining birth rate, and passage of tax limitation propositions in some states have been noted by Chabotar and Honan (1990, p. 28) as contributing pressures to hold institutions of higher learning both accountable and affordable. While providing strategies for coping with institutional retrenchment, these researchers suggest that redefinition of mission is a significant factor in adjusting effectively to changes in the external environment.

Definition of purpose, or mission, is attributed to the development of an organization's strategic plan. Since the introduction of strategic planning in the corporate world in the 1970s, institutions of higher education, and other nonprofit entities as well, have embraced this concept as a means not only to better communicate goals, but also allocate resources. The mission statement has become the symbol of strategic planning and the management literature is rich with research, analysis, and how-to guidelines for its development. The relationship between the stated purpose or business of an organization (its mission) and the culture of an organization (its values, beliefs, and aspirations) is suggested by many researchers to be critical to organizational success, longevity, and distinctiveness.

Given real and imagined threats to today's academic library (distributed computing, redundant instruction curriculum, expanded study, and recre-

ADVANCES IN LIBRARIANSHIP, VOL. 21

0065-2830/97 $25.00

ational centers), the fact that the mission of college and university libraries is not often well understood is a significant problem. How do mission statements play a role in clarifying the purpose of the academic library within the broader institutional framework?

Like their parent institutions, many college and university libraries have identified strategic planning and formulation of mission statements as tools to improve stature within the enterprise. Institutional initiatives in strategic planning, accreditation reviews, and increased campus competition for declining resources have emerged as the predominant reasons for libraries to begin development of more explicit statements of mission. What are library mission statements saying about what we do and how we do it? An analysis of the literature and an examination of California college and university library mission statements reveal a variety of descriptions of purpose. In addition, when considered by type of institution, or institution by institution, the college and university library values studied do not present a clear, focused set of beliefs connecting the library to institutional distinctiveness.

While the library profession is infused with ethics and codes of professional conduct, external constituents of the library often do not perceive what business the library is in (its mission) nor how it practices its mission (through values). Could it be that libraries as organizations are overlooking an opportunity to communicate and promote those educational values deeply rooted in their parent institutions? Had libraries effectively communicated their mission and values over the years, winning the "hearts and minds" of the communities they served, positioning for more resources and campus visibility would not have become the necessary library management strategy.

This chapter identifies the characteristics of effective mission statements as gleaned from the business and library science literature, examines a sample of college and university mission statements for values language, interprets the success or failure of these library mission statements to communicate explicit values and beliefs, and recommends a new approach to the development of statements of purpose, specifically through the articulation of values within both library and institutional mission. It is concluded that college and university library mission statements would improve their effectiveness if a cultural (values, beliefs, meanings) frame of development were considered either in addition to or in place of the typical strategic (mechanical, structural) frame of development.

II. Mission, Values, and Vision

A. Background

Drucker (1994, p. 96) claims that every organization has a theory of the business. The theory of the business is based upon assumptions about its environment, market, clientele, technology, mission, and the core competencies needed to accomplish the mission. Evolved from his earlier works, he suggests that the relationship between these factors makes or inhibits an organization's effectiveness. Specifically, Drucker and others have suggested over time that a business cannot successfully survive without identifying its mission. There is a difference, however, between simply identifying mission as compared with communicating and believing in the mission. Drucker suggests that the theory of the business, if articulated in a clear, consistent, and focused manner, has tremendous power. The power to create a more effective organization can only be realized if the theory of the business, or mission, is well understood throughout the organization and its greater environment. Finally, Drucker asserts that it is the believed or perceived theory of the business that becomes the culture of the organization. It is the culture of the organization—not just *being* the organization—that is distinct and unique.

Institutions of higher learning are rethinking, reengineering, and restructuring to claim the competitive edge. Rising tuition, declining enrollments, increasing technology costs, and insufficient outside funding have all forced the modern college and university to look to its unique purpose or mission as key to securing position in the marketplace of the academy. While statements of purpose or mission describe the "education" business of the enterprise, savvy marketing directors are pushing the academic administrator to capture the essence of how his or her campus offers a "value-added" educational experience. This marketing strategy suggests that an organization can gain a competitive edge when its culture and values are clear and distinct from those of other institutions.

Where do the college or university libraries fit into this larger institutional picture? Do their mission statements likewise make explicit the value-added elements of library competencies, resources, and services? Unfortunately, college and university library mission statements in general do not.

B. Definitions

1. Mission Statements

Definitions of mission statements are generously represented in the management and library science literature. The most basic definition of a mission statement is that it is a written statement describing an organization's reason for existence. Hardesty and colleagues (1988, p. 12) offer the definition of mission statement as the mechanism by which the organization communicates its overarching and fundamental purpose. Woods (1988, p. 13) states that mission statements are those core documents which tell why an organization exists and what it aims to achieve. However, a close examination of the literature reveals more multidimensional definitions. The Hardesty article notes that long-term philosophy and aspirations can be elements of mission statements. In the Jones and Kahaner study of 50 corporate mission statements "that hit the mark" (1995, p. ix), these authors define mission statements comprehensively as the "operational, ethical, and financial guiding lights of companies. . . . they articulate the goals, dreams, behavior, culture, and strategies of companies." Brophy (1991, p. 137) adds such descriptors as "value-laden and behavioral" to his definition of mission, noting that statements of values are less common than statements of purpose. While definitions strongly suggest that mission statements by association express values or cultural norms of an organization, several researchers observe that the latter are found—if at all—in other written documents (e.g., internal policy documents, or the more recent but less common, vision or values statement). Robinson (1994, p. 30) suggests that library documents other than mission statements are important to examine when seeking statements of values given the observation that limited ethical topics were identified in most library statements of purpose. Her analysis of the mission and code of ethics statements, and strategic planning and policy documents, of 120 Association of Research Libraries member libraries revealed conservative use of values language. She notes that rather than having derived these statements from institutional uniqueness, they typically adopted language from professional associations such as the American Library Association.

2. Values Statements

Values statements per se are less common than mission statements. Researchers note though that successful organizations articulate what they hold to be important, and thus, examination of the question "what are values?" is instructive. Values, simply stated, are thought to be ideals which people believe to be important, worthwhile, and good. Examples of general values are respect for the person, honesty, integrity, social responsibility, excellence, and innovation. Values reflect a general code of behavior stemming from a corporate philosophy, according to Morris (1996, p. 109). Silvers (1994, p. 12) suggests that mission is just one element in an organization's communication about itself. Values and beliefs form the core or foundation of an organization; purpose or mission is thought to be the obvious. Silvers maintains that people often find mission statements uninspirational because they do not focus on the more compelling belief structure of an organization. Silvers highlights the often cited management researchers Bennis and Nanus, who in 1985 describe differences between leaders and managers. Leaders, as distinct from managers, they maintain, operate on the emotional and spiritual resources of the organization (values, commitments, and aspirations).

Brabet and Klemm (1994) offer an intriguing hypothesis about the role of values as compared in companies strategically oriented (British organizations) versus those more culturally oriented (French organizations). Strategically oriented organizations, Brabet and Klemm suggest, do their corporate thinking at the management level. Mission statements in these organizations are primarily written by managers, an observation also noted by Hardesty. These statements are usually based only upon the company's core purpose, product, and technology. Values do not surface as a critical organizational characteristic. On the other hand, businesses in France tend to be more employee driven, thus collaborative corporate thinking and planning has produced value-based structures. Extended employee participation in French organizations has influenced the process of mission statement development according to these authors because personal values influence shared corporate values. When infused with expression of values or beliefs, mission statements become symbolic.

Symbols represent or communicate distinct organizational culture. They are important because they inform, educate, and inspire. Symbols have the potential of explaining meaning, creating interest, motivating people to engage or act; thus contributing to perception of value. Many researchers maintain that when an organization has *perceived* meaning and *explicitly* expresses it, then that organization has a better chance of being successful. Being successful can position an organization to stand out distinctly in the marketplace. As noted earlier, institutions of higher education are busy trying to communicate how their missions—to educate—are unique enough to make significant differences in the lives of their students. A library mission statement might likewise communicate how library services and resources contribute to the total learning experience within the particular culture of its parent institution.

In a text used by Harvard's Graduate School of Education as part of the Management Development Program, authors Bolman and Deal (1991, p. xiii) make the observation that "organizations that are overmanaged but underled eventually lose any sense of spirit or purpose. . . . we need leaders and managers who combine hardheaded realism with a deep commitment in values and purposes larger than themselves." Bolman and Deal suggest four frames of thinking which they believe offer a potentially powerful strategy for organizational effectiveness. When integrated across an organization, these conceptual frames encourage thought, inquiry, and action into these areas of organization: people (human relations), power (politics), structure (organization), and symbols (cultural). The authors maintain that the leader or manager who understands the power of symbols (representing basic values or beliefs) has a better chance of influencing the organization than one who only focus on the other thinking frames (e.g., political or structural). If this is so, then it would follow that communicating *meaning* or *values* in what an organization says about itself could affect how that organization functions distinctively.

3. Vision Statements

Having a vision statement in an organization has emerged in the media and in the workplace as an important ingredient for the development of a successful enterprise. In recent years, the literature notes how articulation of vision in addition to mission and values is a trend observed in the language of corporate documents. Where it is true that some organizations make a clear distinction between expression of mission, values, and vision, other organizations do not. For this reason, research which employs content analysis of mission statements may or may not include organizational vision or belief language if embedded in its other documentation as noted earlier.

Vision as it relates to organizations is defined by Block (1987, pp. 108–109) as "our deepest expression of what we want . . . a vision is the preferred future, a desirable state, an ideal state. It is an expression of optimism despite the bureaucratic surrounding or the evidence to the contrary." Silvers states (1994, p. 10) that "vision is a picture of what a leader wants their organization to become. It [the vision] focuses on end result, not how to get there." Silvers maintains, however, that merely having the vision is not enough. The vision must be founded on core mission, values, and beliefs. Quigley (1994, p. 39) suggests that a leader's ability to create an effective organization happens by translating a vision into reality through demonstration of actions and behavior framed by organizational values. Value-based action and behavior commonly triggers like action and behavior. When employees choose to emulate organizational values in this way, the expressed vision of the business becomes tangible and understandable. Jones and Kahaner's recent study on mission statements (1995) observes that those organizations that try to live up to stated vision and values are the most successful and exciting companies in corporate America. This is notable because these companies make the effort to achieve their mission *in the right way* as defined by a set of values. Finally, statements of vision do not appear as frequently as do statements of mission, values, and beliefs in the documents analyzed by Jones and Kahaner. This could suggest that vision, while important, is not as critical to organizational effectiveness as are values.

III. A Study of California College and University Library Mission Statements

A. The Study

In 1995, research was conducted to study California college and university mission statements in order to examine the extent to which libraries in these organizations articulated values. The mission statements of 4-year college, university, and specialized institutions of higher education were solicited.

Two-year institutions were not included in the study. Of the 104 mission statements requested, 65 libraries responded. Fifty-eight mission statements were received with 7 respondents indicating that no mission statement existed for their organizations. Of the statements received, 5 included explicit values or vision statements as well. Several libraries noted that their organization was engaged or about to be engaged in a revision of the document as part of broader institutional planning. This research sample of 62.5% was analyzed for content, specifically for language which expressed a value or values. Data was organized by nine institutional types as defined by the Carnegie Foundation for the Advancement of Teaching, *A Classification of Institutions of Higher Education*, 1994 edition. These institutional types fall into the general categories of *research*, *doctoral*, *masters*, *baccalaureate*, and *specialized* (see Appendix A).

B. General Observations

The mission statements of California college and university libraries gathered for analysis reveal a variety of expressed purposes and values. Library missions, regardless of institutional type of organization, were most often characterized as "supporting the educational mission, curriculum, and research of the institution." Developing collections, teaching information skills, serving as a gateway to global information, and providing a physical learning environment were also frequently noted as important elements of organizational purpose. When examining these college and university library mission statements for values language in the aggregate, libraries as organizations appear to have a rich and complex array of values or beliefs which inform their structures (see Table I). However, when mission statements are examined by institutional category, or institution by institution, it is less clear how mention of certain values communicate a particular philosophy about its unique "theory of the business." The description of values as analyzed does not present compelling evidence that library mission statements define and support a strong values-based culture within the organization. Analysis of the data suggests that there exists fewer distinct elements of institutional culture between and among different types of libraries (i.e. research, doctoral, masters) than is commonly perceived. While the Carnegie definitions of institutional type offer tangible characteristics which make them different from one another (number and kind of degrees offered, funds received to support research, etc.), the statements of purpose and values as expressed in the library mission statements do not suggest that college and university libraries differ significantly from each other in mission or beliefs.

C. Analysis of Data

Table I summarizes the 22 values gleaned from 58 California college and university mission statements, including those described by specialized col-

Table I Values in California College and University Library Mission Statements[a]

	Universities				Colleges				
	Research		Doctoral		Masters		Baccalaureate		
	I	II	I	II	I	II	I	II	Specialized
Lifelong learning	●	●	●	●	●	●	●	○	●
Quality/excellence (teaching/service)	●		●	●	○	●	○	●	●
Diversity			○	○	●	○	○	○	○
Critical thinking	○	●	●	○				●	○
Leadership	○		●	●		○		○	○
Public service/common good	●	●		○	○	●		○	
Student centered	●			○			○	●	
Scholarship	●	●	○	○					
Collaboration	○			○	●				○
Effective use of resources					○	○			●
Innovation	●				●	●			
Energetic service	○				○				○
Dynamic organization	○			○	○				
Adult learners								○	●
Faith				○				○	
Integrity						○		○	
Academic freedom				○	○				
Open communication	●							○	
Forward looking	●				○				
Creativity							○		
Inspiration									○
Institutional history			○						

[a] The symbols of the table are defined as follows: (●) value noted in two or more mission statements for this institutional category; (○) value noted in one mission statement for this institutional category.

leges or universities. The values are listed in descending order starting with the value mentioned by all 9 institutional categories to the value noted by only 1 institutional category. The table also indicates those values mentioned by 2 or more libraries as compared to those where values are noted only once in a mission statement. What is interesting about the data is the fact that the values expressed in the sample do not suggest any consistent pattern or association between institutional category and perception of institutional culture. While certain expressed values do correspond to the mission of a particular type of institution, there appears a randomness to values articulated across college, university, and specialized libraries.

The values most frequently cited in the college and university mission statements studied were:

lifelong learning
quality and excellence in teaching and service
diversity
critical thinking
leadership
the common good and public service

The general value of lifelong learning was mentioned by every type of library regardless of its institutional category. Commitment to quality teaching and service was the second most frequently cited value across all but one institutional category. While these statements of value are relevant to the educational mission of each library's parent institution, these two specific values do not necessarily articulate a unique quality about the library which could be said to connect it to institutional distinctiveness. Lifelong learning could, for example, be promoted in the mission statement as a primary and explicit value when linked to a distinct institutional value. If critical to a particular institutional mission, this value could be described in terms of how its library teaching curriculum contributes to strong and sustainable student learning skills for use in the workplace. In this way, the value of lifelong learning has the potential of expressing a cultural, less generic set of beliefs. When articulated in a way that enables people to imagine how lifelong learning and libraries play a role beyond higher education, this value takes on meaning to the individual that might suggest how a particular institution offers a value-added orientation to its education.

Diversity, critical thinking, public service, and the common good were among the values cited by the larger number of institutional types. However, at close examination the frequency with which each value is expressed and type of library by which the values are mentioned raise questions regarding what is being communicated about the organizations. For example, diversity is noted as a value among all types of libraries except for research institutions. Yet the mention of diversity occurs only one time for each institutional category. The value of diversity does not appear to be a dominant value for all doctoral, baccalaureate, or specialized institutions in the study, but rather a value for just one library in each category. In contrast, several libraries from masters I institutions (offering 40 or more masters degrees in three or more disciplines) identified diversity as an important value. The fact that institutions placed in this category range from large public universities to medium-size private colleges may explain the variety of libraries seeking to include the value of diversity within their mission statements. This does not, however, explain the absence of the value diversity in the mission statements of larger, more comprehensive institutions. If in fact diversity is a significant ingredient in California library organizational culture, the mission statements studied do not suggest a clear relationship between this value and library programs or resources. How these programs and resources contribute to the particular meaning of diversity within the parent institution (i.e., curricular diversity, ethnic diversity within the student population, etc.) is not presented in the mission statements as a distinct goal or outcome.

The occurrence of the value critical thinking also raises questions about how libraries characterize a particular value as one central to their mission. In the study, the value of critical thinking is mentioned in the mission statements of research, doctoral, and specialized institutions. Interestingly, critical thinking has been identified and promoted in higher education as a learned skill primary to the mission of teaching institutions. Yet those institutions associated with a teaching mission did not as a general rule include the value of critical thinking in their mission statements.

Of the remaining values identified by most of the nine institutional categories, public service or dedication to the common good was expressed by more than one library for research and masters I-type institutions. While it follows that public service would be a key element in the mission statements of large public research institutions, it is less clear why doctoral and masters institutional libraries would not also identify public service as an important value. The fact that this particular value is expressed by two or more masters II libraries might suggest the emergence of the common good as a value noted not by association to the constituency served, but rather by religious or faith-oriented traditions embedded in institutional affiliation. However, because the language used was not explicit in relating the common good value to broader institutional mission, expression of this value cannot be said to create an intentional or unique organizational culture. Specialized libraries did not express public service or dedication to the common good in the sample.

Many of the values identified in the study were expressed by three to four institutional types, usually receiving mention by just one library in a given category. These occasionally stated values were:

scholarship
student centered
collaboration
effective use of resources
innovation
energetic service
dynamic organization
adult learners

In this list of values, the occurrence of scholarship as a value for libraries supporting research and doctoral programs is consistent with the primary mission of those institutions while masters, baccalaureate, and specialized libraries do not express scholarship as an organizational value at all. Beyond scholarship, however, the values of student centeredness, collaboration, effective use of resources, innovation, energetic service, dynamic organization, and adult learners are noted sporadically with little or no apparent relationship to institutional category. For example, the value of student centeredness has a perceived association with a teaching organization or institution. Yet, the mission statements studied showed an absence of student centeredness as a stated value for the teaching–masters I or II institutional libraries. Student centeredness was a value expressed for several research I institutions, one doctoral institution, and one or more libraries at baccalaureate institutions. The study suggests that defining an organizational culture which focuses on the student is not only the purview of the teaching college; nor are the libraries associated with teaching institutions promoting this value as one which distinctly influences its mission within the larger organization.

Many institutions of higher education identify adult learners as a primary student population for whom the educational service is designed. As a stated library value in this study, however, service to the adult learner was not identified by any research, doctoral, or masters-level institutional library. Specialized libraries did express educational support of the adult learner. This is consistent with their institutional mission, one dedicated to such distinct professional oriented disciplines such as the fine and practical arts, chiropractic, psychology, and marine science. Because degree programs for adults are a distinct market in higher education, the lack of communicating an organizational culture tailored for this constituency suggests a missed opportunity in defining specific library mission.

Unlike the typical values described in business or corporate mission statements—integrity, creativity, inspiration, and having vision—the analysis of California college and university mission statements revealed limited mention of these kinds of values when describing library organizational culture. Table I notes the following values expressed in two or fewer institutional categories, usually mentioned by only one library within each category:

faith
integrity
academic freedom
open communication
forward looking
creativity
inspiration
institutional history

While library managers might recognize the need to identify values which communicate particular ways of implementing their mission consistent with the culture of the institution, library mission statements in general do not convey how organizations carry out their purposes in distinct or unique ways. Achieving mission through action and behavior influenced by cultural values such as integrity, open communication, and creativity has been suggested by the researchers cited in this study as a method which contributes to organizational success and effectiveness. This study generates little evidence from its sample that values have been communicated in a way which creates a distinct culture within organizations. Although the study did not analyze institutional mission statements, the dearth of explicit cultural values in library mission statements suggests a potential weakness in the effectiveness of professional communication about the role of libraries in the broader institutional setting.

IV. Conclusion

A. Implications from Research

The relationship between the stated purpose or mission of an organization and the culture of that organization has been suggested by researchers to be critical to organizational success, longevity, and distinctiveness. The identification, communication, and perception of values or beliefs within an organization creates a cultural framework from which an organization can effectively achieve its mission. Furthermore, researchers suggest that the mission–values dynamic is not often found in organizations which function from merely a structural or strategic orientation; instead, either a collaborative or cultural organizational orientation characterizes successful enterprises.

In an analysis of California college and university library mission statements, language which expressed a value or values was found across research, doctoral, masters, baccalaureate, and specialized institutions. The values identified in general did not closely associate the academic library with the particular mission or values of the parent institution, nor were the values articulated in such a way to communicate how library resources or services contribute to the distinct educational product of the larger organization. Although the library mission statements convey a purpose within the organizations, the college and university libraries sampled do not express a unique culture between or among differing types of libraries. While this study did not undertake to determine whether the libraries were successful within their institutional culture, it is concluded that these college and university library mission statements do not explicitly contribute to organizational effectiveness given the ambiguity of values expressed in relation to their perceived institutional association.

Colleges and universities are examining how their missions offer distinct educational experiences in the marketplace of higher education. The role of the academic library within each institution as a perceived value-added academic resource could contribute to overall organizational effectiveness. Understanding of, and belief in, library mission *and* values has the potential of creating an educational culture associated directly and uniquely with the broader institution. Researchers suggest that a well-crafted mission statement can position an organization for success when it includes language that communicates values and beliefs that show people meaning. The purpose of many organizations may be the same. It is the manner in which they choose to conduct business that determines uniqueness. Today academic libraries are being challenged about the meaning and relevance of their services and resources. To express in clearer terms why the culture of the library has value to the college or university appears to be one solution in assuring organizational effectiveness, longevity, and distinctiveness. Using the mission statement (or whatever is determined to be the core symbolic document of meaning) to articulate distinct library culture is suggested only when it also embodies the values of the organization and of the larger institution.

B. New Approach to Mission Statement Development

The business literature suggests that the key elements of organizational mission statements include purpose or reason for existence, the values intended to inform how the purpose is achieved, and vision to which the organization aspires. Given that college and university libraries are organizations within larger institutions, the values of the parent organization are critical in shaping its library services and resources. Because the study of California library mission statements in general does not provide evidence of explicit and unique culture, a new approach to mission statement development is suggested. Academic libraries should consider collaborative development of distinct library values within and connected to institutional mission. A mission statement is most useful when it articulates why a particular college or university's education would be less than distinctive if its academic library was not perceived to be an essential organizational culture.

Appendix A

Definitions of Institutional Categories[1]

Research Universities I

Offer full range of baccalaureate programs; committed to graduate education through the doctorate; give high priority to research; 50 or more doctoral degrees awarded per year; receive $40 million or more in federal support per year.

Research Universities II

Offer full range of baccalaureate programs; committed to graduate education through the doctorate; give high priority to research; 50 or more doctoral degrees awarded per year; receive $15.5–40 million in federal support per year.

Doctoral Universities I

Offer full range of baccalaureate programs; committed to graduate education through doctorate; at least 40 doctoral degrees awarded per year in five or more disciplines.

Doctoral Universities II

Offer full range of baccalaureate programs; committed to graduate education through doctorate; at least 10 doctoral degrees awarded per year in three or more disciplines **or** 20 or more doctoral degrees in one or more disciplines awarded per year.

Master's (Comprehensive) Colleges and Universities I

Offer full range of baccalaureate programs; committed to graduate education through the master's degree; 40 or more master's degrees awarded in three or more disciplines per year.

[1] From *A Classification of Institutions of Higher Education*, 1994 edition, The Carnegie Foundation for the Advancement of Teaching.

Master's (Comprehensive) Colleges and Universities II

Offer full range of baccalaureate programs; committed to graduate education through the master's degree; 20 or more master's degrees awarded in one or more disciplines per year.

Baccalaureate (Liberal Arts) Colleges I

Primarily undergraduate colleges with emphasis on baccalaureate degree programs; 40% or more of baccalaureate degrees are awarded in the liberal arts fields; restrictive in admissions.

Baccalaureate Colleges II

Primarily undergraduate colleges with emphasis on baccalaureate degree programs; less than 40% of baccalaureate degrees are awarded in the liberal arts fields; less restrictive in admissions.

Specialized Institutions

Offer baccalaureate, master's, or doctoral degree programs; 50% or more degrees awarded in single discipline; common discipline specializations are fields of religion and theology, medicine, and other health, engineering and technology, art, music, design, law; other specializations.

References

Block, P. (1987). *The Empowered Manager: Positive Political Skills at Work* (Jossey-Bass Management Series). Jossey-Bass, San Francisco.

Bolman, L. G., and Deal, T. E. (1991). *Reframing Organizations: Artistry, Choice, and Leadership* (Jossey-Bass Management Series; Jossey-Bass Social and Behavioral Science Series; Jossey-Bass Higher and Adult Education Series). Jossey-Bass, San Francisco.

Brabet, J., and Klemm, M. (1994). Sharing the vision: Company mission statements in Britain and France. *Long Range Planning* **27,** 103–115.

Brophy, P. (1991). The mission of the academic library. *British Journal of Academic Librarianship* **6,** 135–147.

Carnegie Foundation for the Advancement of Teachin. (1994). *A Classification of Institutions of Higher Education,* Technical Report. The Carnegie Foundation for the Advancement of Teaching, Princeton, NJ.

Chabotar, K. J., and Honan, J. P. (1990). Coping with retrenchment: strategies and tactics. *Change: A Magazine of Higher Learning* **22,** 28–34.

Drucker, P. (1994). The theory of the business. *Harvard Business Review* **72,** 95–104.

Hardesty, L., Hastreiter, J., and Henderson, D. (1988). Development of college library mission statements. *Journal of Library Administration* **9,** 11–34.

Jones, P., and Kahaner, L. (1995). *Say It and Live It: Fifty Corporate Mission Statements That Hit the Mark.* Doubleday, New York.

Morris, R. J. (1996). Developing a mission for a diversified company. *Long Range Planning* **29,** 103–115.

Quigley, J. V. (1994). Vision: How leaders develop it, share it, and sustain it. *Business Horizons* **37,** 37–41.

Robinson, S. R. (1994). Library mission and codes of ethics: A content analysis of research library policy documents and their ethical premises. Master's Paper, Graduate Program in Library Science, University of North Carolina at Chapel Hill.

Silvers, D. I. (1994). Vision—Not just for CEOs. *Management Quarterly* **35,** 10–14.

Woods, L. B. (1988). Mission statements, organizational goals, and objectives. *Arkansas Libraries* **45,** 13–17.

Index

Cumulative Index for Volumes 17–21

ISBN 0-12-024621-X

90051

9 780120 246212